## DEDICATION

To my children, Michelle, Monica and Michael, and to my two

Grandsons Devan and Dillon. They kept pushing for the "stories" to

end up on paper.

To Heleen, my wife of 48 years, goes the biggest thank you. Until I

wrote these stories, I had no idea just what you have gone through and

put up with.

# Contents

# VIETNAM STATISTICS
## HELICOPTER PILOTS DEATHS

2200 K.I.A (killed in action)

1255 WARRANT OFFICERS

THE AVERAGE AGE OF ALL K.I.A WAS 25 YRS.

THE YOUNGEST K.I.A WAS 19 YRS.

## NON PILOT CREW MEMBER DEATHS (crew chiefs and gunners)

2716 K.I.A

## TOTAL HELICOPTERS IN VIETNAM

11827

## HELICOPTERS DESTROYED

3300 UH-1 HUEY

132 CH-47 CHINOOK

147 0H-13

1507 OTHER

## EVERYDAY IN VIETNAM, HELICOPTER CREWS EARNED MEDALS FOR BRAVERY. SOMETIMES THEY WERE EVEN AWARDED THEM.

# PRELUDE

I was laying there in the weeds, too young, dumb, and full of cum to be scared. I was just 21 years old, but I had been at war for almost a year, flying helicopters around the mountains and jungles of South Vietnam.

I had just managed to crash land in a pond full of snakes. No one had any idea where I was, and I did not have a clue how I was going to get out of this predicament. Maybe, I will get naked and see if that attracts any attention.

# An Loa Valley

# SNAKES IN THE LAKE

One of our on- going missions was to fly what was called a First Light Recon. I would take off at the first sign of day break while it was still half dark, and fly the jungle trails leading back into the mountains. I was currently flying for E/82$^{nd}$ Artillery, 1$^{st}$ Cavalry Division and had an OH-13 strapped to my ass. E/82$^{nd}$, the Woodpeckers, is the support unit for the Division Artillery. I normally flew reconnaissance for the Infantry soldiers, providing eyes for them from above. If they got into trouble I could bring the big guns from nearby fire bases into the fight, by calling in the grid coordinates of the enemy, and then adjusting the impact of the rounds. Other times I would scout an area of potential enemy hideouts and camps, and then call in the artillery to destroy it.

I was stationed at LZ Two Bits which is right rear Highway 1. Hwy 1 runs from the south of Vietnam up to North Vietnam and was the country's major roadway. The LZ had an airstrip and was a Green Beret camp for quite a while. It sat on a hillside above the village of Bon Son and to the south is the Song Lai Giang River. That river got its start to the west from runoff in the steep mountains surrounding the An Loa Valley. The land around Two Bits was rice paddies and jungle. There were a few hills scattered about and the U.S Army usually staked claim to these. To the west are the mountains and the V.C and NVA laid claim to those.

The enemy soldiers would come down out of the mountains during the night and either stay in a village or set up ambushes on U.S troops. They would hold political meetings or perhaps assassinate a villager loyal to the South Vietnamese Government. The NVA and VC would collect rice and other food, and gather up new recruits or conscripts. They would then head back to the mountains, and their camps in the jungle.

I pulled this duty just about every day and had my routines down pretty good. I usually had this big 2nd Lt. "Griff" who would fly with me. Normally Griff would carry an M-60 machine gun and his job would be to put down suppressive fire if we ran into trouble. Then he got on the radio and either called in artillery fire or got us help. The length of the mission was usually two hours as that's how much fuel the -13 carried, and I had a general area of assignment. I would take off while everyone else was still sleeping except for maybe a crew chief of two, and head out toward the jungle and mountains. One of my favorite hunting areas was the trails leading from the Bon Son plains, back toward the An Loa valley. The An Loa was the scene of many battles, and a lot of the enemy were living up there.

We took off at about 5:30 as the sun was just starting to make an appearance and headed southwest toward the hills. I flew these missions at tree top level or lower. Any higher and I risked getting shot down. I was slow and noisy. My only defensive capability was to be in the trees or grass, where the enemy couldn't see me until I was right on top of them. The funny thing about helicopters flying in the jungle and mountains is that you can hear them, but you cannot really tell just where they are. The noise bounces around, and seems to be coming from everywhere.

I started working trails and streams but was not finding anything so I turned northwest toward the An Loa. I crossed over some small hills leading to the mountains, then dropped down into the valley, and headed for the river that runs down toward the sea. I wasn't in the valley more than a mile when I came across a small lake next to the river. As I got over the top of the water I looked down, and floating on the surface was maybe half dozen very large snakes. I guess they were either boa constrictors, or something related. These snakes were probably anywhere from four to ten feet long, but looked a whole lot bigger.

They were all up on the surface of the lake catching the early morning sun and maybe breakfast. I had more than my share of run-ins with snakes, and I didn't like them. For all I knew they had a huge intelligence network, and knew all about me. They had been tracking me ever since flight school, so I decided now was time for payback. I told Griff, "Shoot the snakes." Griff racked the bolt of the M-60 to make sure he had a round seated, and pointed the machine gun down at the snakes. Well bless my soul, "Karma" reared its ugly head. The engine on my helicopter took this opportunity to quit working, and from about five feet in the air we went "splash."

I was wearing fatigues, a helmet, and a .38 revolver, plus a .22 automatic pistol and a large knife. I also had on my flak jacket and chicken plate. The chicken plate is a twenty pound vest with a bullet proof plate in the front. I had a bandoleer of M-16 magazines strapped across my shoulder, and various heavy items in my pockets. What this all added up to, was to turn me into a rock, when we started sinking in the lake. I also had the M-16 tied to the door, which was blocking my exit, and those snakes are all gathering to attack.

I looked at Griff and he looked at me as we sank into the water. I was 5' 11" and Griff is 6'3" so the last thing I saw as I went under is Griff's shoulders and head up in the fresh air. The -13 sank completely and then miracle of miracles floated back up. There was air trapped in the top of the bubble giving us about two feet of clear air, and the two gas tanks are half full, and also providing flotation.

I stared at Griff and thought the snakes should like him better because he's bigger, plus he was the one that was going to shoot them. Before I could finish this thought, Griff was out and gone, and a moment later I saw him crawling up the bank and into the tall grass.

I was now all alone with the snakes. I shed my gear, and then made like an Olympic free style gold medalist, and within seconds I was laying next to Griff in the weeds.

We took stock and between the two of us we had a pistol each and some ammo, and I had a couple of grenades in my pocket. The M-16 and M-60 sank, along with bullets, beans, smoke grenades and a survival kit. Everything happened so fast, that I didn't have time to make a radio call. No one knew where we were, and we were not expected back for at least an hour.

Now that I knew the snakes couldn't get me, I took inventory of our situation, and figured we would have to "E and E" (escape and evade) back to our base. LZ Two Bits was down river about 10 miles from where we crashed, and it was going to be a long and scary walk back home.

Griff went to Officer's Basic where they taught him how to be an infantryman, before he went to artillery school. He had to have learned map reading, and how to patrol along with classes in survival. Of course, all that wonderful information was nowhere to be found inside his head, at this particular time. As we lay there I couldn't help but think that every enemy soldier within twenty miles, saw the helicopter go down. I figured they were all on their way to either shoot me, or take me to North Vietnam as a P.O.W.

A whole bunch of artillery fire started going over our heads, and landing west of us in the An Loa. ARA (Ariel Rocket Artillery) flew over and started shooting rockets into the jungle. It was a major air assault, and we would not be far away. Then came about twenty four Hueys loaded with grunts that will be dropped into the jungle. Preparing the way was the gunships, which were escorting the troop ships. Two or three things can happen once the troops are on the ground. They can set up patrols and eventually walk our way. They could chase the enemy east bound, in which case we are a two man blocking unit Or they can find nothing going on, and load up and go back home. I just didn't know which of the three I was going to get.

The troop Hueys headed back toward LZ Two Bits, and then I saw one of the gunships flying low level down the river. Griff and I were lying in the tall grass between the lake and river. I had a twenty-one year olds, inspiration. I stood up and threw a grenade into the river in front of the gunship. This gunship had a grenade launcher in the front, and rocket pods and machine guns on the sides. It also has a crew of four, two of which are in the back with M-60 machine guns. For all they knew, they have just been attacked by a crazy V.C. The gunship didn't deviate from its path, and no one seemed to look to see why a geyser of water should be blowing up in their path. I waved and jumped up and down, but nothing happened. How all four of the crew failed to see me is a mystery. They just continued flying down the river. Only later did I start thinking how dumb an idea that was. The gunship crew could have blown me away.

My next tactical plans called for me to strip naked, except for my boots, and then get out to the helicopter to see what I could salvage, before we started our "E and E" trek. The helicopter was bobbing peacefully not far from shore, and the blades were angled toward the bank. I figured that I could jump down on the mudflats and then swim a short distance to the helicopter blade, crawl out and get inside. Part of my plan also involved opening the fuel tanks somehow, and then when all done, I would throw my last grenade inside the helicopter to blow up the radios and make the helicopter sink.

I looked around and could not see the snakes anywhere so I launched myself off the bank, and down to the weed covered mud flats. Now I found where some of the snakes had gone, when their little lake was invaded by the H-13. They again took off, while I screamed like a ten year old girl and tried not to die of heart failure. I jumped into the water and swam like crazy to the blade. I crawled on and shimmied my way out to the helicopter, and got up on top of the engine, between the fuel tanks.

I heard the distinctive whop-whop-whop of a Huey, and looked up. A helicopter was flying back to Two Bits, and passed over me at about 1500 feet. I later learned that one pilot said to the other pilot, "Turn around and go back. I think I see a helicopter floating in a lake." Of course, he was met with, "Bull shit. What have you been smoking?"

They did turn and made a low level pass over me at which time number one pilot said, "See! I wasn't imagining things and I think there is a naked guy sitting on top."

I walked on water to get back to Griff, and the helicopter crew called for help, then started to set down near us. I thought the Huey was out of control because it was moving all over the place, and I was worried it was going to crash. It looked like all the controls had gone spastic. It was just those two pilots were laughing so hard, they couldn't fly the damn thing.

A Ch-47 Chinook was requested to pull my helicopter out of the lake. That big twin rotor beast could lift anything. A Chinook landed shortly and a rigging crew got my H-13 ready to be lifted back to base. When they were going to start the lift, they loaded us on board, then hovered over the -13 and hooked up. They pulled it out of the lake and headed back to Two Bits. When we arrived it made quite a show, because my -13 had picked up this long grass from the lake, and it was hanging down looking like some kind of hula skirt. The Chinook dropped the bird on the runway, and moved off a little to set down and unload me and Griff. The ramp lowered and we walked off with all these people standing around watching. I had gotten re-dressed, but as I walked across the runway I was squeaking because my boots were so waterlogged.

# THE EARLY YEARS

Ironically, a vivid memory of those early years was of playing army with all of the neighbor kids.  We lived on a nice middle class street of single family homes. The vacant lot across from our house became the battle field. We spent hours and hours digging trenches and fox holes, and then having imaginary battles with the enemy. I can't remember where we got our equipment, but we all had real army helmets and web belts with ammo pouches and canteens. This wasn't too long after WWII and Korea so it probably came from neighbor's basements. All of us kids also had our own B.B guns which only added another dimension to the combat. Little did I know what the future would hold for me.

I was born in Minnesota, but a few years later we moved to Washington State. Minnesota was my mother's home state, and she had met my father there. He was passing through while still in the Navy and I still haven't figured that out yet. As a kid there, I lived near my grandparents and great grandparents. All the families lived near Medicine Lake which was not far from Minneapolis. My mother, father, and I lived in a small log cabin in the woods, and next door was a large two story log cabin where my great grandparents lived.

When I was four we packed up and moved west to Tacoma which was my father's home town. At that time, in the late 40s, Tacoma was the third largest city in the state, and was a blue collar town of about

140,000 souls. My dad was going to go into the produce business with his father.

Mom worked off and on but mainly had kids and took care of the house. I always think of her as June Cleaver. If she wasn't in the kitchen making breakfast, lunch and dinners she was standing over the ironing board. Every damn thing in that house got ironed, and she is still doing it today. The sheets; pillowcases; all the clothes; the drapes; my underwear; and socks. It didn't matter. If it could be ironed, then it got ironed. I never saw her actually put an extension cord on the iron and do the couch and living room carpet, but it wouldn't surprise me.

Mom is probably 5' 2" and 100 pounds, and that is if she puts rocks in her pockets, but she never slows down. Even today I'll call and ask her how she is doing and she'll respond that her back hurts or her knees. I then have to go through twenty questions to find out why. "Well, I pulled out the refrigerator and dusted because it's Tuesday. And not one of my children was around to help me dig up the tree that needed to be moved. And I had to get the ladder and take down the curtains because they hadn't been ironed in over a week, but I'm fine. Don't worry. Maybe a nice neighborhood boy will come over and help me."

Dad had his own produce store and worked from sun up to sun down. Besides selling produce to walk in customers, he had a route and delivered fruit and vegetables to several restaurants. When I got older I would work with him on the weekends once in a while, but I wasn't much help. He would load his panel truck up with sacks and boxes, and crates of vegetables and fruit, and away we would go.

He would double park in front of a restaurant and grab two, fifty pound sacks of potatoes and tell me to get one and haul it inside. At that time the sack probably weighted about ten pounds more than I did. He'd have a sack under each arm and I'd be trying to get my one sack out of the truck and onto the side walk. He'd laugh at me and so would all the customers watching. I remember being humiliated, and that stuck with me all the way through childhood and my teen years.

I was the oldest of what was to become five children, so I was the one on which my mother and father learned their parenting skills.  Kids just don't come with a training manual, so it's on the job training. It was a pretty steep learning curve to get any of it right. Throw in emotional problems, drinking, and youth and it's no wonder parents are in over their heads. When I was born my mother was just twenty, and my father was twenty one. I look back to when I was twenty and a new father, and I have no idea how I ever got through it.

My biggest problem growing up was that I felt my Dad hated me and of course those feeling became reciprocal and I hated him. I don't think he had a clue as to how a father should act toward his son. When I was growing up it seemed like it was a daily ritual of being yelled at. There never seemed to be peace. My father would work, drink, yell, and fight with my mother or my brothers and sisters. My post teen and teen years were filled with bad memories, but in reality were probably no worse than anyone else. It seemed like everyone's father was cooler or smarter, or more laid back than my own, but I really didn't know what went on when I wasn't around their home.

I tried everything to fit in with the other kids. I joined the Boy's Club and played baseball and football. I look back on those years, and I am reminded by the team pictures how small I was. I also don't remember a single time my father attended a game. We lived near a large city park that was the site of all the practices and games, and it was within walking distance of our house. I just have no memory of him ever being there. I am sure he was busy trying to earn a living.

I was always being picked on by the other kids both in the neighborhood and at school, so I got the bright idea to take up boxing. I signed up at the Boy's Club and started taking lessons from the coach. I'm sure I had visions in my mind of becoming a real boxer and then being able to clean the clock of the kids who were bullying me. I faintly remember also thinking that I could stand up to my father, if I became tough enough.

It wasn't too long into our training program and sparring, when we were told that we would be having a boxing match with another Boy's Club. The real clincher was that we would travel by boat across Puget Sound, and put on the bouts at McNeil Island Federal Penitentiary. On the day of the matches we loaded into an old school bus, and drove to the small town of Steilacoom, which is located on the shores of Puget Sound. We all walked down the dock and climbed aboard this 40 foot boat crewed by prison guards. There were about ten of us kids and a couple of adult coaches.

We arrived and were escorted by guards into this huge auditorium. There must have been a thousand prisoners sitting there, and the ring was set up on the stage. We had prisoners acting as the referee, and other prisoners were assigned as our assistants in the corners. I remember being scared to death, and when my bout started this crusty old criminal kept yelling at me to go out and kill the other kid. I ran out to the middle of the ring and just flailed away until he gave up. I didn't want to have to go back to that corner and face that prisoner again. I was temporarily scared straight at the age of twelve. Too bad it didn't take.

I never wanted to go to school, and when I did, I did not pay attention. I was smart and always passed the tests, but cannot remember ever carrying a book home, or doing home work. I skipped more days in high school than I ever attended. Of course I was also staying up late every night to watch Steve Allen and then sleeping in class the next day.

I wanted to have friends and be popular, but no matter how hard I tried it just didn't seem to be my destiny. I had started school at a young age, so I was almost a year younger than everyone I was in school with. They all got cars before me, and of course they were older and more mature. When I was in grade school I was tormented by my class mates and saddled with the nickname, "Baby face." Try spending four years like that. Going to school every day knowing you will be mocked, not to mention being shoved around and on occasion hit. Now that I think back, I guess baby face is not so bad. At least I was not being called Mule, Lavern the Biscuit, or Stinky like some of my classmates.

I attended a Catholic school run by the Nuns. These were big intimidating penguins with a thirty pound Rosary hanging around their neck ,and a wooden ruler concealed inside their habit. You cannot believe how quick on the draw those ladies were. They would be standing twenty-five feet away from me, with their back turned, and I'd try and sneak a piece of gum out of my pocket. Whack! "How in the hell did she do that?" I still have indentations on the back of my fingers from that steel edged ruler. I also heard that they had little holes in the back of the wimple, and that is why they could see you, even if they were facing the other way.

In the Seventh grade I signed up for and was accepted to be an altar boy. Our church had a couple of priests, and one of them was older than dirt. All of the day to day stuff was handled by Father Norris, who was much younger. Father Norris had come from Ireland by way of New York City. I was told that he had been in trouble and prison in Ireland, and when he was released, headed for the U.S.A. He became a longshoreman in New York before seeing the light, and taking his vows as a priest. The problem was he still talked and acted like he was a longshoreman.

I would dress in my floor length black Cossack and then put on a white surplice, and as I readied to head to the altar, Father Norris would hand around the bottle of sacramental wine, and we would all take a healthy pull. At that age it went right to our heads, and I served several masses with a buzzing in my noggin.

Father Norris also liked to play golf on Saturdays, but he only played at Pacific Lutheran University. I always got invited along to be his caddy, and the two of us played alone. He would get to the first tee and then open a beer and light up a cigarette. He would hand both to me and tell me not to touch either while he hit his drive. He would stand there and peer down the fairway, waggle his driver, and generally kill enough time to insure I got a few puffs off the cigarette and about a quarter of the beer. If my mother had ever known about this, she would have gone to hell for killing that priest.

Father Norris would happily smack golf balls all over the course, and after he had had a couple of beers, he would start anointing the trees and bushes. Every time he whipped it out to spray, he would start yelling, "Piss on the Lutherans." I was always thankful we were out there alone.

I got so desperate for friends and especially female attention that there was only one course of action open to me. I wrote a love letter to Annette Funicello. I had been watching her on the Mickey Mouse Club every day for a year or so, and I now noticed that somehow she had gotten bumps in her Disney sweater. If only she would write back and tell me everything was going to be great, and maybe include a picture of her with an autograph, I could take it to school for show and tell. Then who would be the coolest kid in Seventh grade? But it was never to be. I tried to beat my mother to the mailbox every day so no one would find out. No letter came back. Nor a picture. I am still holding a grudge and refuse to watch re-runs of Beach Blanket Bingo.

By the time I turned into a teenager, the family had grown and with three bedrooms we were cramped for space. My father converted a corner of the basement into a room for me and I gleefully set up my private space. I immediately discovered the one major drawback. I was about fourteen, and my parents were twenty years older. My bedroom was directly beneath their room. I remember the first time. I was laying there and all of sudden the ceiling above me was banging and dust was falling out of the rafters. What in the hell is going on? *OH!*

I also had the same experience when my son was about eight years old. He wanted to know why our bedroom door was always locked, and how come we did not fix the squeaky rocking chair.
*"Go turn on the T.V. and watch cartoons."*

In my teen years I would often bring a friend over on Friday after school, so that I could angle toward going out to a dance or a party. My father would wait until the last minute, and then tell me I could not go. He was always in the humiliation mode. All of my friends either had their own car, or they got to use the family sedan on a weekend night. I would ask to use the car and be told no. Then he would change his mind, and tell me I could have the car, I just had to arm wrestle him for the keys. He was near six foot and 200 pounds of muscle and I was five feet something, and skin and bones. The outcome was predetermined. He would sit there smirking at me, and then tell me to use two hands. I still couldn't beat him, and at that point he would tell my friend to help me. Rarely did we take his arm down, and of course I would not get the keys.

I was little for my age and at graduation from high school was probably 5'7" and 130 pounds. I had plenty of dates and never lacked for female company, but still managed to be the only guy I knew, who graduated from high school a virgin. I did not see a naked woman until the time I stumbled into an art class in college. Even then I was chased off before I got a good look.

I spent my entire formative years never hearing the words "I love you" from my father. Later in life I became a Warrant Officer and helicopter pilot in the U.S Army and served two tours in Vietnam, and then spent a total of twenty-eight years in the military, retiring as one of first CW-5s when Congress created that new rank. I also spent a total of thirty-five years in Law Enforcement. I retired from the Tacoma Police Department as a homicide detective, and then retired again as a fraud investigator with the State of Washington. I cannot recall my father ever telling me he was proud of me, or my accomplishments.

I struggled when I became a husband and father, and it took me a very long time to break that pattern of behavior. Only in later years did I come to understand that this was all due to post traumatic stress disorder. My father had been in the Navy in WW II and served on aircraft carriers in the Pacific. He was just sixteen years old years when he enlisted and left high school to join up. He shortly turned seventeen and was shipped out to the war.

He never mentioned anything about his service, and I never heard him tell a war story. In later years I learned he had served on CV-9 "The Essex". He was a tail gunner on a TBF Avenger, which was a torpedo bomber, and was shot down in a battle somewhere in the South Pacific islands. I asked my mother if he had ever mentioned the war, and she replied that he very seldom said anything. The only thing he would recount were his stories about his buddies, and the misadventures they got into while in some port like Honolulu.

I have no idea what he may have seen or experienced, but in retrospect all of his behavior patterns showed he probably had PTSD. Violent mood swings; hair trigger temper; fights with the family, or in a bar; always shying away from social encounters. He had it all, and at one time I thought I had simply inherited those traits.

I sit here today, as I have often done, and wish that I could have a do-over as a father. All those years I spent following in my father's footsteps. I tried my best to make up for those times, but I was often reminded by my wife and children that I did not make life very pleasant for them. The worst part is now knowing, that if I had only been diagnosed early, then maybe things would have been better.

# I'M OFF TO JOIN THE CIRCUS

When I was fifteen I finally got a car. Not to drive, but to work on until I was sixteen and could get a driver's license. It was a sweet little '50 Chevy, two-door hardtop, that had belonged to an uncle. I bought it for $100, and right away started fixing it up. It was painted salmon pink, and had a white canvas top.

I had to have money for all of the revisions I was going to make, so I was always looking for an odd job, or a full time position doing something. During this period I believe I went through about twenty different jobs in one year. I don't remember all of them, but I do remember the shortest. Dennis, Rich, Pat and I went looking for a way to make money and stumbled on a job opening at the local chicken factory. There was a sign out front with a help wanted notice, and we applied. They sent us out back to a warehouse, and we spent the entire day doing inventory on all the material stored there. There were cartons and cartons of paper wrap; boxes of plastic trays; advertising materials; and everything that was needed to package and ship chicken. When we were finished for the day the boss paid us in cash, and then told us he had one position open starting the next day, and who wanted it. The other guys agreed that I was the most in need of money, so they gave up the job to me.

The next day I showed up bright and early wearing white Levis, a white T-shirt my mom had ironed, and white tennis shoes and socks. I was led around back, and found myself standing with a bunch of guys dressed head to toe in rubber. They had a long rubber apron on, with elbow high rubber gloves; plus rubber boots and a hat. It was then I found out that my new job was to pull live chickens from the metal cages. I had to hang them upside down on a hook by their feet, and then slice their throats. It seemed the chickens knew what was coming because they didn't make it easy. They would all crowd into one corner of their wire cage, and flap their wings like crazy. Pretty soon the air was full of flying feathers, blood, and chicken shit, and it was all sticking to me. I lasted thirty minutes.

I walked off the job and started home. About one mile away lived an aunt and uncle, so I figured I would stop there and get a ride home. I knocked on the door and my uncle opened it, took one look at me, and closed the door. He then shouted at me to head around to the back. He met me there, took his garden hose and began spraying all the chicken parts off. When he was finished he gave me a towel, loaded me into his car and then drove me home. I never did get my final pay check from that company.

Of course, life continued as it was with my father and I being at odds, until I reached the point where I knew I had get out. So one night I took the blankets off my bed and laid them in the driveway by the garage. The driveway was gravel and I did not want to alert anyone that I was leaving. I then pushed my car out of the garage and down the alley, until I reached a spot where I could start it. My next stop was to pick up the other idiot that was traveling with me, a kid named

Dick.

This was a period in my life when I was attracted to trouble. It seemed like I was always around when someone would do something stupid, and I never had enough sense to avoid these people. One time we were walking in an alley looking for pop bottles, so we could return them for the deposit. There was a pinball arcade that we all hung around, and of course it was eating up our allowances. The next thing I knew, Dick is flying past me and yelling, "Run." I did not know if someone was chasing us or just what was happening, so I took off after him. We went about three blocks and finally stopped, and I asked him what was going on. He pulled a purse out from under his coat, and told me he had taken it from a car in the alley. I panicked and made him stuff it down a sewer grate, and then we headed to the arcade.

I thought about what had happened, and finally made him go back to retrieve the purse. We walked back to the house where he had stolen the purse, with the idea of putting it back in the car. When we got there, the cops were waiting and arrested us both. Later he admitted that I did not know about the theft, and I was released.

Another time I got in trouble with Dick was when I had a paper route. I had to get up at 5:00 a.m. to deliver the Sunday papers, and he went along to keep me company and help out. It was cold and damp and I would often get the papers ready in an all night Laundromat. I was rolling papers and sticking them in my carrier, when I saw Dick spray painting the washers and dryers. I told him to quit and left him there while I went to make my rounds. On Monday morning I got called into the principal's office at my high school.

Waiting for me were the cops again. It seems that Dick not only spray painted the machines, he also wrote his and my names on the wall. It did not take much detective work to figure out who was responsible. Again he admitted that I wasn't involved, but I ended up having to repaint the walls in the laundry, and scrape the spray paint off the machines.

I hated to lose that paper route. I was finally making steady money. In those days I would deliver papers every single evening and then on Sunday morning. At the end of the month I had to collect the money owed from each household, and then I had to pay the newspaper for the papers I had gotten from them. I had one house in particular that I loved to deliver to. This family all worked except for the nineteen year old daughter, who was in nursing school. Almost every night I would stop by her house and she would teach me interesting things such as, "This is how you French kiss. Girls really like that. Today in school we learned how to make an erection go down. Want to see how that works? We had anatomy class today and these are called breasts. Here, touch them so you know what they feel like." *I think you might have to make the erection go down again.*

It got so the papers were being delivered to the rest of the houses, later and later each night. Now that I think about it, I don't remember ever collecting from her house either.

I picked up Dick and we went around local neighborhoods, siphoning gas out of every car we could find. I remember sucking a lot of gas that night through a garden hose, and getting sick because of it. I had a four foot piece of hose and a gallon jug. I had to suck gas and fill the jug. Then I had to empty the jug into the gas tank, and repeat the process. I did all the dirty work, and Dick provided look out duties.

I do not think we had $5.00 between the two of us, but we were off and running. We traveled to eastern Washington, and joined a traveling carnival and rodeo. The carnival was owned by Johnny Meeker, who also owned Johnny's Dock Restaurant in Tacoma. The company also had a manufacturing plant where they produced Johnny's Seasoning Salt and Au Jus and other products, but I do not get to buy at a discount. You would think as an ex-employee, I would be entitled.

This traveling cast of misfits consisted of carnie games and rides and went everywhere the rodeo went. Why they would hire two runaway kids is anyone's guess but hire us they did. We fit right in with the rest of the motley crew.

I was assigned to work in a game booth, and was taken over by the boss, to meet the lady that ran it. She was old. Maybe somewhere around 21 and wise beyond her years. "Hi there hansom. Stick around and I will show you some tricks". I spent the next couple of hours with her showing me all the tricks of the business, and how to get people to lay their money down. The suckers bought three wooden rings for a $1.00, and had to toss them over the top of coke bottles. In the middle of the booth were several dozen cases of empty bottles. The bottles were packed tight and the rings were just barely large enough to fit over them. I would take a ring and show the sucker how it would lay right over the top of a coke bottle, and if he got one to stay on, I would give him a stuffed animal. I never saw anyone win at this game on their own, but once in awhile someone was allowed to win. There was nothing better than having a girl walking around with a big stuffed bear or tiger, for good advertising.

I was taking as much money as I could from the game when the boss lady wasn't looking. I don't remember how much they were going to pay us per hour, but I knew it wasn't going to be enough to put gas in the car or find a place to sleep. I would get a $5.00 or $10.00 bill, give change to the customer, and put the large bills in my socks. We had no place to stay, and no food to eat, plus I knew I had to do something about the car I was driving.

That little '50 Chevy was painted a real nice salmon pink. I figured every cop in the state was looking for it, and I had better disguise it. Later that afternoon my boss told me we're closing up, and that if I needed a place to stay, I could come back later and sleep in the game booth. It was like a tent with wooden sides and canvas that rolled down to enclose it. It also had a canvas roof and was about ten feet on a side, so it was very roomy. This seemed like a great idea.

I drove to the nearest auto parts store and bought a gallon of black primer, and two whisk brooms. Later that evening I parked in the rodeo arena, and Dick and I painted the car. It was an extremely nice paint job except for the broom marks, bits of straw stuck to the sides, and the primer on the chrome. *No one will ever figure this camouflage out.*

When we were finally finished, I was tuckered out. We had driven a lot to get to where we were, and then worked all day in the game booths. I had finished work, only to spend a couple of hours painting the car. I hadn't eaten all day, but could only think about bedding down and getting some sleep. I headed for the game booth, and when I arrived, found a line of approximately eight to ten men standing there. I had no idea what they were doing at my new home, so I joined the line at the end. About every ten or fifteen minutes the group would move up a little, but there was no one behind me, and I just kept my place in line. After a while the man in front of me turned around, looked at me, and just started laughing. This guy was wearing a plaid shirt with the sleeves rolled up and a pair of those farmer overalls, and I couldn't see many teeth in that mouth. He spit a gob of something black and then poked the guy in front of him and pointed at me. Now the two of them were laughing. He finally asked me, "What are you doing in the line, kid?" and I said, "I am waiting to get into the game booth, because that's where I am sleeping." They just laughed harder and then the farm boy said, "You have no idea what is going on, do you?" I got tired of this and figured it would be a while before I was going to get any sleep, so I went back to my car and curled up in the back seat and slept there.

We spent the next couple of days in Ellensburg, working the booths and helping out with the rodeo. Everything was then packed up, and we caravanned to Moses Lake, to set up there for a weekend run. All of these towns had their annual rodeos, and they were spaced out so that they would run for a few days. Then we would have a couple of days to move to the next town.

In Moses Lake there were now three of us hanging out together, so we pooled our money and got a motel room. We were all tired of sleeping on the ground or in the car, so we thought we were owed a bed and shower. I was pretty sure we needed the shower.

This was where I found out you could get ride tickets from the carnival guys, and use them to lure farm girls into the Tunnel of Love, or onto the Ferris wheel. The older guys were filling our heads with stories about getting to touch boobs, or even doing "the deed" in the hay barn. I had always been shy, and so no matter how many ride tickets I got and used on the local farm girls, I never got more than a kiss or two. I was sure those girls were a lot more advanced than I was, but I just could not connect the dots.

On our first night in the motel room we were sitting around smoking and joking and acting like big shots. All three of us were young. I was fifteen and Dick was sixteen, and our new roommate was seventeen or eighteen, but none of us seemed to have a clue. Suddenly there was a banging on the door and when I answered it, there stood this mountain of a man. He had a case of beer under each arm and bags of ice at his feet. The giant was "Hoss Cartwright" who was just getting started in the TV show Bonanza and he was doing the rodeo circuit. I remember him looking at us and saying, "You fellows aren't using the bathtub are you?" With that he walked in and dumped the beer and ice into our bathtub, turning it into his own ice chest. He started drinking beers and gave us a couple, and then he informed us he needed a place to sleep and was going to use one of the beds. So we ended up with Dan Blocker as a roommate that night, with two crammed into the other bed, and I was on the floor with a pillow and the bedspread.

A few days later we packed up again and the three of us jumped into my car for the next stop on tour. This was the city of Yakima. I remember starting out on the drive, but I was so tired that I just could not handle it. We stopped at a diner for food and gas, and it was suggested that I take some "NoDoz" to keep me awake. Of course it had the opposite effect and I was nodding off before we went five miles. The older kid then got behind the wheel, and I got into the back seat to sleep.

The next thing I knew, I had a light shining in my eyes and a policeman was asking me my name. We were arrested and hauled to the Yakima Police Department. I learned that the guy driving, was an escapee from the boy's reformatory, and that he panicked when he saw the police car, and made a left turn in front of the cops. They pulled us over, identified him and placed him under arrest, and then started looking for who else might be in the car. By that time the check on the license plate showed that it was reported stolen, and that the arch criminals, Michael and Rich, were wanted by the Tacoma Police Department.

We were taken to the Yakima county juvenile detention center. I was told to empty my pockets and strip down to my under wear. The hard case next to me whispered that I should hide a couple of cigarettes up my ass, because they were going to take them away from me. He did not explain where I was supposed to hide the matches. I figured that I would give up smoking at this point.

Next on the list of instructions was, to inform us that we would be marched into the common area three times a day for meals. We were to put our head down, with our chin on our chest, and not look up for any reason. It was explained to us jail birds, that after we were seated, they would march the girls in from the other wing. Most of these girls were in for prostitution and they did not want us to be able to recognize them on the street. We were threatened with a head thumping if we were caught looking up.

Now you just know we all tried to get a peek. I knew what a prostitute was, but had never seen one in real life. So there I was at every meal, trying to see through the tops of my eye lids. I finally managed to get a look, only to see several ugly Indian women. The guards could have made everything easier on me, by just showing the girls in the first place. One look and I never wanted to see them again.

The cells were one man units with concrete walls, floor and ceiling. The cell contained a hard cot, and a sink and toilet. I had no television or radio, or even a magazine to read. And definitely no one to talk to. There was one small window that looked out at another building, and a steel door with a tiny screened window, set high up. If I stood on my tip toes I could see the wall across from my cell. Absolutely nothing to do all day except wait for the call to meals. This was the longest three days of my life, and finally my parents showed up to take me home. I think by this time, I even liked my father. Or at least I did for this one day.

Life returned to what it was, and I continued being who I was. Nothing spectacular. After being gone for about three weeks, I returned to high school, but it seemed no one had missed me. I was not on any sport teams, and did not participate in any school activities, except for the ski club. I had no high grade point average, or any dreams of a college scholarship.

I later joined the wrestling team and as I like to tell the story, I was never beaten. After a few weeks of practice we had a match against another high school. I was wrestling at the 125 pound weight. My match started, and I grabbed the other kid, threw him down and jumped on him to get the pin, and win. I didn't use any move I had learned in team practice, but had reverted to something I had seen on *"Rasslin."* It was the *"Flying Ass Grab,"* or the *"Pancake Pile Driver"* or some such crap, but it had the other kid totally confused. After I finished my match, I snuck outside to have a cigarette. I no sooner lit up a smoke, when Doc Christensen, our wrestling coach, caught me and threw me off the team. Technically, I remain undefeated.

# D. BOONE

*I next became a motor cycle outlaw.*

We were all back to looking for ways to make money, and Dennis told us that he had a neighbor who wanted his house painted. The deal was that the neighbor would buy the paint and materials, and four of us would paint the house for $200, to be split evenly.

Paint the house we did, plus the drive way, some of the windows and trim, and of course each other. It wasn't pretty, but it was done. I got my share and faced the options of saving the money, spending the money on parts for my car, or blowing it on something frivolous. Yep! Guess which option was chosen?

There was this brand new dealership in Tacoma called Honda, and they had these cute little 50cc scooters for sale or rent. They were the red, step through models that did about 45 m.p.h. The four of us rented one each for the weekend, and after the check out, we're told to stay within the city limits of Tacoma. We immediately hit the freeway going southbound, with a destination of Seaside, Oregon which was about 180 miles away. The four of us had those little scooters wound up and redlined and doing about 50 m.p.h on Interstate 5, with every car in the world passing us. The vibrations were killing our butts, so we could only ride about an hour before we had to get off and walk around.  For every hour we rode, we had to rest for an hour. I had absolutely no feeling below the waist, and my hands and arms were tingling.

We spent the entire day getting to Seaside, and knew we had to have the motor scooters back the next day. So we made one pass down the main drag, turned around and headed back for home. We slept in a field, next to the bikes that night, and made it home the next afternoon. The guy at the Honda dealership couldn't believe we put 500 miles on the scooters riding around Tacoma, but we stuck to our story.

I drove fast cars, greased back my hair, pegged my pants, smoked and acted tough, but was anything but. I continually stuck my nose where it didn't belong and of course got it broke about three times by guys who took offence. "Hey! You three guys can't do that to that guy!" POW! A broken nose.

There was a time when I was really attracted to this girl in my class. She was dating another guy at the time, but that didn't keep me away. I heard her current boyfriend talking to another guy, and he was saying how he was going to get this girl drunk, so he could have sex with her. Stupid me. I told her. She told him. He took me out behind the school and I got another broken nose.

The last broken nose was the result of a misunderstanding. Another girl told me that she had broken up with her boyfriend. She was babysitting, and would really like some company. I arrived, and was just getting comfortable, when the boyfriend showed up with two other guys. The girl had failed to tell him she no longer wished to be going steady. I got invited out to the alley behind the house, and did not even get to put up my dukes. Another swollen snot locker and blood all over my new Christmas shirt.

I was also a ski bum during this period. Actually it started in high school with me skiing with my best friend Rich Steen. His family did everything together, and I got to join right in. We water skied all summer, and snow skied all winter. I used to skip school and head up to Mt Rainier with my skis. Of course being the rocket scientist that I was, I couldn't figure how I kept getting caught by the school for skipping. Then I found out that the teachers would notice that I was always sunburned after being away from class sick, and the only place to achieve that was above the clouds, up on the snowy slopes.

I had the ski bum business down to a science. I would put a $1.00 worth of gas in a friend's car while they were in school, and then drive to a small town called Sumner. I would park behind a barber shop and grab my skis and standby the highway. Pretty soon someone headed for the mountains would pick me up, and drop me at the ski slopes. I shoveled snow for a free lift ticket. At lunch time I would go through the garbage cans and find an orange, a couple of cookies or a half a sandwich. I never went hungry.

At the end of the day I hitchhiked back to Sumner, or found someone staying in a cabin and would sleep on their couch. If I wasn't proud I could spend an entire weekend skiing, and never spend more than a

$1.00 or $2.00.

It was during these times when I may have developed an addiction to nudity. Seems I was always pulling down my pants and mooning someone, or ending up naked sleeping in a snow bank. Why I was naked doesn't seem to ring any bells, but I'm guessing beer may have had something to do with it. Anyway, Mom must have heard a rumor or two, because for Christmas that year I opened a present from her that contained a full length red flannel night gown. It had a whole bunch of buttons that started at the neck and didn't end until the ankles. It even came with a nice matching stocking cap. At least if I froze to death I would be looking good.

I also discovered that I really liked the Limbo. I was in the ski club at school, and all of us would rent cabins or a lodge for a weekend of skiing. There were probably about twenty of us in the club, and if we had chaperons, they seemed to disappear whenever we got to the evening's festivities. We were in the lodge at Mt. Rainier one time and had a fire roaring in the big rock fireplace. Someone went and got a pole, turned on the music, and a line formed to do the limbo. The pole kept getting lower and lower, and kids were being eliminated when they couldn't get under it. I was sitting on the hearth watching everyone trying to get under the pole in front of me, when I noticed a really strange sight. Marie had on cute little shoes and socks. She had on a cute little skirt and blouse. What she didn't have on was any cute little underpants. There was this huge hairy animal staring at me, and I stared right back. I called Pat over and told him about my discovery, so he joined me on the hearth. We kept yelling at Marie that we just knew she could get under the pole, and that she should keep on trying. Finally, some dumb girl noticed what we were doing and told Marie, so she quit before we could crown her the Limbo Queen.

Now don't get me wrong. All of these life lessons were great training aids for later in life when I became a cop. I remember when I applied to become a police officer and they were looking at my life history, and interviewing everyone I knew. One of the sergeants remarked that I was a great candidate because, "It takes one to know one," whatever the hell he meant by that.

But all of that was in the future. I still had to get through puberty. My nuts hadn't dropped. I couldn't grow a mustache. I still weighted somewhere around 130 pounds, and I was really anxious to get laid. I think that between age fourteen and eighteen, is when I developed carpal tunnel syndrome, which would require surgery in later years. Good god! I was yanking on that thing ten times a day. My permanent date was, "Miss Thumb and her four Finger Sisters." I think I even bent it. Now it hangs down, and always points at my left shoe, which has caused me to hook my tee shots.

I finally graduated with a whopping 2.0 grade point average and no prospects. I enrolled at a Jr. College in Bremerton, and Rich, Pat and I moved there to share an apartment and get an education. I packed my clothes and helped myself to my parents' extra kitchen table, which was stored in the basement. I also took the bamboo roll up shade off the living room window. I just happened to be in my "Oriental Period", and knew these items would come in handy.

The three of us rented an apartment in the basement of this large building. It had the usual kitchen and living room, plus a bath and two bedrooms. One of the bedrooms was very large so Rich and I shared it. The bamboo curtain got hung from the ceiling to provide a barrier. The kitchen table found its way to the living room. I cut off the legs so they were about a foot long, and then I painted the table black. My living room was now a Japanese tea house, and I got a sore back, sitting on the floor and eating. But I was looking cool.

Of course trouble was still following me around. One night Rich and I had a few beers with the neighbors, and then we all headed out to walk around town. It was cold so I borrowed a coat from Pat McNeil, my other roommate. He was not home because he was working at Safeway as a night stocker. I just knew he wouldn't mind me wearing it.

As we walked around town the neighbor guys were getting rowdy, and the next thing I knew, one of them threw a flower planter through the window of a business. There was a janitor inside, and he saw us and called the cops. Rich and I ran home and hid in our back bedroom. Within minutes of us hiding, Pat came home from work, and had just taken off his shoes, when there was a knock at the door. Pat opened it to find two cops standing there. One looked in the living room, and then asked Pat if that was his jacket sitting on the couch. Pat said yes, and the cops grabbed him and hauled him to jail. Positive I.D. provided by the janitor, who said he would recognize that jacket anywhere. Pat finally convinced the cops to call Safeway, and the manager there verified that Pat had been at work all night. So they let him go, and never did figure out who the guilty parties were. Pat wouldn't talk to me for about a week.

A couple of weeks later we were sitting around the campus sub building, when a few guys we knew, came in and stated bragging. They had been on their way to a drive-in movie on Friday night, when they spotted a girl walking down the highway. Being smart asses, they pulled over and asked if she wanted a ride. She asked where they were going, and when they said the movies; she hopped in the back seat with one of them. Anyway, one thing led to another, and she had sex with all three, and was now living with them in their apartment. Plus, anyone who wanted to, could go over to their apartment, and she would have sex with them too. Pat didn't care to go, because he had been jumping up and down on his girl friend for about two years. Rich and I were still virgins, and figured this would be the perfect time to correct that situation. I mean here was a girl that was more than willing, and you did not have to spend your money, or even kiss her if you did not want to. So Rich and I started making plans to go over there the coming weekend.

Before our big day arrived to go to the apartment, we were told that the girl had left and hitched a ride to Tacoma, where she apparently lived. A few days later, one of the guys showed up with an article from the Tacoma News Tribune. It told the story of a fifteen year old escapee from the girl's reformatory near Bremerton, who was found at a house party and re-arrested. Guess who?

About a week went by, when all of the original three guys came down with the clap. This was followed by numerous others, and I think the final count was a total of thirty-five guys. Rich and I were eternally grateful that we didn't make it to the apartment, but that didn't stop us from laughing at the guys who did. We made them sit by themselves at the, "Table of Shame" in the school cafeteria.

All of this higher learning lasted one semester. The school called me in, to inform me that I didn't really need to return for the next semester. I had barely attended a single class, and mostly majored in partying. So back home I went.

At this point it was mutually agreed by my parents and I, that a change of scenery was in my future. I was packed up, and put on a train to Minnesota to live with my grandparents. I had also been sent to live with them after I graduated from the eighth grade, and stayed for about nine months and attended school there.

Minneapolis was light years ahead of Washington State in terms of dance, dress and appearance. I showed up with skin tight blue jeans and a shirt with the collar turned up in the back. I carried a rat tail comb and had slip on wedgies shoes with steel cleats on the bottom. The other kids picked me as an outsider right away. Minneapolis kids were into the preppy look with slacks and cords and button down shirts. They all wore their hair cut short, with a side part. I had naturally curly hair, and kept it in place with a lot of Brylcream or Butch Wax. The clothing change was easy, but the hair was going to present a problem. My grandmother said she had a solution, and so every night there I was smearing some type of hair gel onto my head, and then covering it with a nylon stocking. I would get up in the morning and head for the bathroom. Off would come the nylon and I would look hopefully for my hair to be lying flat. Nope. The minute the stocking came off, all the curls popped right back up. I finally had to have it cut so short, that it didn't stand a chance of curling.

We lived in a small town north of Minneapolis called Robbinsdale. My grandfather use to take me hunting and fishing and it was during this time when I learned many valuable lessons.

The first lesson was never ever fire a gun that someone has just handed to you unless you first inspect it. My grandfather took me pheasant hunting, and provided me with and over and under .410 shotgun. We were out in this field with a few of his friends, and a couple of dogs, when the birds were flushed and everyone started to fire. I pulled the trigger on that gun, only to have it discharge and immediately break in half. The pin holding the barrel to the stock didn't work and would just fall out. There I was holding a half of a gun while the other half lay in the grass. I got sent to the car to sit while the real hunters discussed my failings.

The hunting tips were followed by boating and fishing skills. I learned the hard way that even though adults chew tobacco, children shouldn't. Especially when I was in a small fishing boat on a big lake. The wind was blowing, and the waves were growing. I chummed that lake for damn near an hour, and I was as green as the lily pads.

The next lesson was that if you kill it, you clean and eat it. I had a .22 rifle to use whenever I wanted and would go out in the woods and target shoot. One day, this ferocious squirrel looked like he might attack me, so I shot him out of his tree. I scooped him up and carried him home by the tail, which I then hung him from on the fence. When my grandfather got home he spotted the squirrel. He told me that since I shot it, I had to gut it and skin it, and then cut it up for a meal. That old squirrel hung there for about a week, because I wasn't going anywhere near it. Finally my grandfather made me go out and take the squirrel off the fence and bury it. That was the last time I ever went hunting.

The final lesson was never catch more fish than you can eat. I went fishing every chance I got. From where we lived, I could walk in any direction just a short distance, and find myself a lake. I had a cane pole with about ten feet of line and a bobber, and would dig up a can full of worms and off I would go. I never came home without a couple of fish.
Usually it was crappies or sun fish and occasionally, something bigger. I would clean the fish, and my grandmother would pan fry them up for dinner.

One day I walked to the lake and set up on the shoreline and just started hauling in sunfish. You would have thought I had stumbled onto a fish farm. My arm finally got tired of casting, and I had twenty-four fish on my stringer. I lifted them up, and had to hold them above my head to keep them from dragging in the road. By the time I finally got home, the ones on the bottom of the stringer were looking pretty ragged from the road rash. Since I was tired I hung them on the fence, and promised I would clean them soon. Later, I went back out and started it on the cleaning. I got through about six or eight fish, and just couldn't stand the sight of them any longer. So back on the fence they went. My grandfather got home from work that night, and spotted the fish so it was lecture time again. The fish hung there on the fence for a few more days, and were starting to stink, so they ended up being buried by the squirrel. That was the last time I ever went fishing, and the last time I ever could eat fish.

My two grandsons, Devan and Dillon hunt and fish and are real out doormen. I surely must have passed on my hunter-killer, Daniel Boone genes to them.

It was a childhood that was really pretty ideal. I would swim and fish all summer, and in the winter every kid got out their ice skates. My grandparents got me a pair of hockey skates so I could join in. I would walk to school carrying my skates, and as soon as classes were over, head for the local park. The town staff would board up the play ground, and flood it with water. The park would freeze and we had instant skating ponds. On the weekends we all met there, and someone would build a fire. Then we would pair up with a girl and skate around and around. All of us trying to show off our skills. I also learned how to play hockey, and did this on a local lake every weekend

I was now back in Minnesota, with nothing but a suit case. I had graduated from high school, and tried college with no success, so after settling in, my grandparents informed me that I needed to find a job. But first I had to have some fun. I started making friends with the locals, and we were constantly into some form of mischief. On Friday nights we hung out at the local American Legion hall where they hosted a dance. I knew how to dance, and I was a new guy in town, so I was in demand. I was still not scoring but I did have a lot of fun. The girls started inviting me to house parties, and I was falling in love/lust about once a week. Most of the girls went to Catholic school, but I was doing my damned best to convert them to sinners. Seems they were too afraid of confession to fall for my line of charm.

This was the dead of winter in Minnesota and everything was frozen solid, especially the lakes. One night we talked Jerry into taking his car out on Medicine Lake and we were taking turns racing across the ice, and doing spins. We finally crashed into the bank one too many times, and wrecked something under the car. So we just left it there and headed back to town. Someone then got the bright idea that we should pool our money, and buy a car and do this again. We ended up with an old '49 or '50 Hudson, which cost us about $20.00 We then procured a battery and some gas, and off we went again. We would be out on the ice, drinking beer and spinning and crashing until the car fell apart. We would abandon it, and figure a way to do it all over again. There are several lakes in Minnesota with cars sitting on the bottom.

Sometimes we would take the cars out on the country roads. We would tie a rope to the rear bumper, and the other end to a toboggan. The smart guy would drive, and the idiots would climb on for the ride of their life. It was crack the whip at 35 m.p.h. We had our share of scrapes and bruises, but no one died.

We were doing this one night and the car hit a skunk. This car was borrowed from one of the guy's mother, and now we know we are going to catch hell. I don't know what the skunk was doing out in the middle of winter, but whatever it was, it came to a rather abrupt end. "Pepe La Pew" was splattered all over the undercarriage and parts were flung in our direction. The car stunk but we smelled worse. We all piled into the car, and whoever was driving stuck his head out the window to get fresh air. Talk about a stinky ride back to town.

The first job I found, was working in a frozen bread factory. This was a two story building where they made bread upstairs, where it was nice and warm. Then sent it down to the basement, where it was flash frozen and packaged. That's where I worked. This was Minnesota, and it was winter, so it's colder than a *witch's tit*. I had never fondled witches boobs, or for that matter any boob, but everyone assured me that they were cold. I had to walk to work because I didn't have a car, so I was freezing by the time I got there. Now I had to go down the basement, where they kept it at about minus thirty- degrees, and package frozen bread all day. We took our breaks and went outside to stand in the snow to warm up. It was probably a fifty degree difference from inside to outside.

I immediately started looking for a new job and found one working at a Henry's drive-in restaurant. Henry's was either a local chain or regional chain. I don't remember which, but I do remember that its competitor was something called McDonalds. The place was located in north Minneapolis, in what was referred to as the "black district". I rode the bus to work for a while. I would get off at a stop about three blocks from the drive-in, and have to walk the rest of the way. At night I reversed the process.

My grandfather and I went car shopping and I found a real nice '54 Chevy Corvette. My grandfather found a not so nice, '54 Ford sedan. This was going to be sort of my car when my grandmother wasn't going to use it, and I figured the Corvette was way cooler. We got the Ford.

The only place I could park the car was out in the street in front of the house, because my grandfather got the garage for his Cadillac. He had to leave early for work, and needed the driveway clear. Every day I had to go out and start shoveling the snow banks to find that car, because the snow plows would come through the streets at night and bury everything. Then I would have to use a blow torch on the oil pan to get the lube moving. No sense warming the car up, as the heater didn't work, so I was layered up with about 100 pounds of clothes. I looked like the Michelin Man and could barely move.

Henry's made me a cook and I fried burgers and made French fries and fish sandwiches. There were two of us "white guys" working there and everyone else was black. No women allowed. The guys working there all lived in the neighborhood, and were a really nice bunch. I started getting an education, and some real life experiences.

On the nights that I worked, we always had two Minneapolis cops sitting in the back room with shotguns. These two guys were huge. One was black and the other a mulatto. They wore these great coats that were wool, and hung down to their knees. They would sit back their eating to their hearts' content. I don't know if the restaurant hired them, or they were just staying off the streets. One night they had been out walking around, and when they returned one of them asked me if I needed a tool kit for my car. He then opened his great coat, and started pulling tool sets out of the inner pockets. They had interrupted a burglary at an auto parts store, and were simply supplementing their salary.

One night the two of them were assigned to a patrol car, and were coming and going on a regular basis. Pretty soon an old Mercury coupe came sliding into our parking lot, followed a few seconds later by the police car. We started hearing popping noises so we went to the back door and looked out. The Merc is at one end of the lot, and the cop car is at the other, and they are trading shots back and forth over the hoods. We ducked down and stayed that way until it was over, and the cops had the bad guys under arrest. My eyes were probably as big as the hubcaps on that Mercury.

Saturday was "whore day". I was told by the guys, that there were about a dozen whore houses within a couple of blocks of the drive in, and on Saturdays the girls would come over for a special treat. They all ordered fish sandwiches and fries and would stand in the foyer and eat and talk. They also loved to sass the white boys. We were being called "honey and sugar" and they would be telling us all the things they could do to us, in exchange for another fishwich or more fries. A whole new education and vocabulary opened up with that job.

Spring finally arrived and I decided it was time to head back to Washington. It was also about this time that I found I was getting married. I had met this girl, and we were dating quite a bit. Then strange things started to happen. She would insist I take her down town to Minneapolis and go shopping. Every store we went into, she would start looking at table settings and dishes. Then she would drag me into the linen departments, and look at bed spreads and sheets. Next would be a visit to the furniture section and so on. This went on a couple of days a week, for two or three weeks. She then sprang a little surprise on me. Seems she had dallied before, and had a one year old daughter, that was currently living with an aunt somewhere in Minnesota. The daughter was now coming home to live with mommy. *"Isn't this exciting?"* This scared me for a while, but then I figured: *"Hmmm, at least I know she has put out before. Maybe I'll get lucky yet?"* Then some mutual friends asked me about the wedding. I said,

"WHAT?" She had started making plans for out little family, and had even started the invitations. Now I know I'm getting out of Dodge.

A week or so before I quit Henry's, they hired a new white guy named Murphy, and made him the night manager. His job was to run the drive-in, and every night he had to lock up and then make a bank deposit. Shortly after getting back home to my parents, I got a call from my grandmother who told me that Murphy was dead. He opened the back door to leave and make a deposit, when he was confronted by a robber. He refused to give up the money and was shot and killed.

## GIRL OF MY DREAMS

I was now back living in my parents' home, and finding odd jobs here and there. One week it's a gas station pumping gas and washing windshields. The next week I'm sweeping and mopping floors at the local Woolworths. None of these jobs lasted, and I just kept moving on. I got back together with all my boyhood pals, and I picked up where I had left off. Every Friday and Saturday night we all headed to the local Armory or the Crescent Ballroom, for dances and girls. The Wailers, Viceroys, Kingsmen, and Paul Revere and the Raiders were all up and coming bands at this time, and I got to hear all their songs before they made the national charts.

I was invited to a party at a girls' apartment. Patty was the girlfriend of a friend, and I was told I could come. I called the girl I was currently trying to round the bases with, and off we went. I walked into the apartment and there before me was my future wife, Heleen. She was sharing the apartment with Patty, and was currently separated from her longtime boyfriend, who was off at college being cool. Heleen and I had gone to high school together, but ran in totally different groups. We just sort of knew each other. I totally ignored my date. which started a crying jag on her part, and I spent the whole night trying to get close to Heleen. Being smarter than I am, she ignored me.

One thing led to another and we soon started dating. It took me a while to wear down her resistance, so she could see what a total catch I was.

This threw everyone, because Heleen only dated jocks that had things going for them, like college and a future. They didn't smoke and drive fast cars and drink beer with their buddies. They sure as hell didn't have greased back hair with a curl hanging down the front, and a ducks ass in the back.

The roommate, Patty was working at Hooker Chemical and told me about an opening there, so the next thing you know, I have a girlfriend and a job. Hooker Chemical was located down on the waterfront in Tacoma, and made things such as chlorine gas. I started as the plant mail carrier. I would drive all over the plant, and deliver memos, plans, messages or anything else that needed to get from point A to B. After a couple of weeks of that I got promoted to the cell operation. Here they made these giant cells out of concrete and carbon blades, that looked like a battery. These cells were used to create chlorine gas. Once they had been used they had to be dismantled, and this was done with a jack hammer. I got to be the jack hammer guy. The hammer weighed almost as much as I did. When I grabbed it and turned it on, it would throw me all over the place. This was extremely funny to the men who worked there. *"What'cha doing there Mikey?"*
*" I'mmmmm jacccccccck hammmmmering"*

I was supposed to pick up Patty every morning and take her to work with me, and I surely tried to do this for a while. But then I would come by to pick her up, and Heleen would be running around in her baby doll p.j's, and pretty soon I was skipping work.
In school I would just get detention. In the real world they fire you. So

there I was looking to marry Heleen, but now I didn't have a job or a pot to piss in.

I also had another problem. A friend of mine had found this drawing in a Playboy magazine, of a cute little blonde, wearing nothing but a sun bonnet. These drawing were done by the artist Vargas, and were in just about every issue. This particular drawing looked just like the girl I wanted to marry. Somehow Mom ended up seeing this picture, and was convinced it was Heleen, and that she had posed for the drawing. Not having seen her naked I couldn't tell if she had, or had not posed. But Mom was convinced, and was not sure she would let her little boy marry this tramp.

# IMPETUOUS

I did find some employment selling shoes in the Mall and I started going to barber school to learn a trade. Heleen's father, Tony, was a barber and ran the local barber school. In 1965 barbers were still cutting hair and making money to live on, and I was reasonably talented enough to get by without slicing someone's ears off. I didn't shave myself but maybe once a week, and here I was shaving people with a straight razor on a daily basis. Heleen had gone to beauty school and was working in a hair salon. We figured we would open our own shop some day with barbering on one side, and Heleen and the hair salon on the other.

The next item on the agenda was to get married and live happily ever after. At 19 years of age we tied the knot and reality struck. What the hell did I get myself into, and how am I going to make this all work. I only agreed to the married part, so I could see Heleen naked and score a home run. Don't tell the kids but I already had gotten to first base.

We had this huge Catholic wedding and that night a reception at a local grange hall. The wedding was held at the same church where I had attended school and been an altar boy. The beer and booze flowed, and everyone danced to a polka band until they couldn't stand up.

There must have been 300 people there, and years later they were still talking about that party. There were kegs of beer everywhere.

Everyone also brought their own bottle of liquor, and we had enough food to feed half of the city. Heleen's father Tony was standing at the door, and everyone who came in got a shot of whiskey just to get them started.

Heleen and I finally made our escape to our new little honeymoon apartment only to find Rich and Pat there drunk. They had snuck over to attach bells to the bottom of the mattress, only to pass out under the bed. Pat had married his long time girl friend, and they were living in the duplex next door, so we got them up and on their way to Pat's.

Married life began and of course I was still acting like the teenager I was. Friends would drop over, and we would party. Or we would go out and then return home, and they would end up sleeping on the couch. Heleen finally laid down the law that we were married, and needed some privacy, and that my friends could go home and sleep.

Vietnam was heating up, but I had no clue about the war. I never studied history in school, but I did watch television. People were getting drafted, and I was registered with the Selective Service Board. I was married but beyond that had no deferments. The chance of me getting called up and going to war was on my mind, but so was the opportunity to do something a little more positive with my life. Heleen's father had been in WWII with Merrill's Marauders and had seen combat in what was then Burma. He advised me that if I was going to be someplace like Burma, which Vietnam was, and that had jungles and snakes and such, that I sure as hell didn't want to do it as an infantry soldier, and be walking around. It was put like this, "Flying is better than walking. Walking is better than running. Running is better than crawling. All of it is better than lying around in the jungle."

So off I went to the recruiters for a little chat. I told the Navy and the Air Force I wanted to be a pilot and they said, "Sure. How much college have you had, and let's see your high school records?" "Well guys. That seems to be where the problem lies. High school is a bit of a blur, and they asked me not to come back to college. Can we just wave those requirements?"

So the next stop was the Army. This recruiter said if I have graduated high school and could pass the entry tests, which were very tough, I could go to Warrant Officer Flight School and be a helicopter pilot. I had never even been in an airplane and was not sure what a helicopter might be, but if I could qualify and pass the tests I was going to become a pilot and an officer all before I was twenty one years old.

# BABY WOC

The first thing I had to do was to take the standardized military entrance exam, which was a long bunch of questions designed to see if you were smart enough to join the army, and go someplace and get shot at. I think you had to get 10 % or so of the possible 150 points to be accepted. If you got 110 points you could also be considered for Officer Candidate School, and if you got more than 130 points you could become a Warrant Officer Candidate, and go to flight school. Real officers hate that when you bring it up. You only have to be somewhat smart to be a lieutenant, but smarter than that to be a warrant officer helicopter pilot.

I scored 140 points and got to have a doctor squeeze by goodies, and ram his really long finger where the sun doesn't shine. Everything seemed to work, including my goodies even after three months of marriage, and a really good effort to wear them out. I was sent to Ft. Polk, LA for basic training. Upon completion of this grueling 8 weeks of running, screaming, crawling, jumping up and down and cleaning everything in sight, I received orders to go to Ft. Wolters, TX for Warrant Officer Candidate (WOC) school, and Primary Helicopter Flight Training.

Another shaved headed graduate and I hitched a ride to Dallas, Texas so we could get a flight home to Washington. We got on a flight which was jammed full. There were uniforms everywhere and most were high ranking officers. Us two sad sacks were sitting there in our baggy uniforms trying to be inconspicuous. The Captain announced that the flight was over booked, and a couple of people would have to be bumped. We looked up, and he was walking down the aisle checking everyone out, until he came to us. He motioned for us both to get up and follow him up the aisle. We got to first class and he stopped, turned around, and closed the drapes separating us from the coach class. The Captain then told us to have a seat. First class was all ours. We were both teen agers, but the stewardess started feeding us cocktails, and by the time we landed in Seattle, we had to be helped off the airplane. This other guy's father was there to pick him up, and was going to drop me off in Tacoma on their way home. He had to pour both of us into the car, where we promptly fell asleep. An hour later I'm standing in my mothers' living room with my bald head, and a Good Conduct Medal. I had every intention of losing that medal as soon as I could get Heleen alone.

Time flew by and two weeks later Heleen and I had to head for Texas. I had Heleen with me and we drove to Ft. Wolters to begin life as military personnel. We stopped in San Francisco on the way south, and picked up a friend of mine from basic training. Mike Ahern and I were assigned to the same WOC class. He had family in Oklahoma and our next stop was to drop off Heleen. She would be staying there with Mike's grandmother and his sister, until I reported in, and hopefully found a place for her to live.

I was restricted to base for the first month and could not live with Heleen. I did find a little trailer in Mineral Wells, and Heleen came down from Oklahoma to join me. She would be on her own until I could start getting passes off base. Heleen lasted one night here, and was so scared that she had to have me come out from base and get her.

One of the other candidates had his family in town as well, and they offered to let Heleen stay there one night until we could find someplace else. This nice family had five kids, and there just wasn't room for a guest. I made my plight known to my Tactical Officer, Wayne Nippert. The TAC Officer was a cross between your mother and the devil. He was there to help you, advise you, discipline you, humiliate you, and make you into a Warrant Officer or wash you out of school for being unfit. TAC Nippert asked around and found a couple of classmates, whose wives were staying together in a house on base. They rated this because they had been in the military for a while, and qualified for on post housing. So, for the third time in three days, Heleen moved again. I was technically stuck in the barracks with all the other WOCs, but the army can't have someone's wife staying in their car or on the street. I got to run off post and move her to the next place. Lo and behold, the other candidates' wives were into parties, and invited some other girls and some guys other than their husbands over. Heleen was hiding in a back bedroom when the M.Ps raided the house, and of course I got another call for help.

Back I went to TAC Nippert with another sob story, and the next thing I know he has Heleen moving in with him and his wife and two children. They were wonderful people and took pity on Heleen's plight, and made her part of their family. Of course this did me no good, as he yelled and intimidated me just like he did with all the other candidates, but he also snuck me to his house for dinner a time or two. Heleen lived with them for a few weeks, until I could get post housing approved, and she then moved into her own little house on base. I immediately had two dozen red roses sent to the Nippert house, as my thanks for everything that they had done for Heleen.

The next morning in formation we were standing at attention and being inspected by Nippert. When he got to me, he leaned over to whisper in my ear, what I was sure was going to be his undying thanks and affection for me. Instead what I heard was, "They should have been yellow. You are on restriction. Now drop and give me twenty-five pushups." Never send a Texan red roses.

In WOC school we had to learn to act like officers, so of course we called these, the "Knife and Fork" classes. You had to be able to attend functions and not embarrass yourself by eating with your fingers, or pouring wine directly from the bottle to your mouth. We had multiple uniforms, and don't even think about getting caught in a wrinkled set of fatigues. Here we are in the Texas heat changing uniforms two and three times a day or "breaking starch". The wives did their part by buying liquid starch and soaking our uniforms in it, and then ironing everything so that the pants and shirts could stand by themselves. Soon, a bunch of us started developing strange rashes in our nether region. It was extremely tough to stand in formation in the blazing sun at rigid attention, when you think your manhood is going to fall off because it itches so badly, and you can't scratch. Turned out the wives thought that everything had to be starched, so in went our t-shirts and underpants also. You just have no idea what misery we went through, until we figured out what the problem was.

Our WOC group was made up of guys fresh out of high school and college, and a good share of soldiers who had been in the Army for a while. Some of this latter group just couldn't handle being bossed around and stressed. They had been in for several years and had earned rank, and just couldn't relinquish this. A lot of them just walked away, and went back to their old units. The washout rate was also affecting the class. This school was tough. It had to be, so that those who couldn't cut it were eliminated before they got to war and killed themselves, or their fellow soldiers. Except for a select few, every single one of us would be going to Vietnam. Within a year this group of mostly teenagers would be flying million dollar helicopters with an array of weapons at their disposal.

The class was getting smaller and you could find yourself on the way out for not being up to snuff in academics, or for not being able to fly. There were virtually no second chances. And do not get caught doing something stupid, like getting arrested by the local police for speeding, drinking, or smoking a little weed.

One group of older soldiers who toughed it out, were Green Berets who had done one or more tours in Vietnam. However, they did think they were above everyone else in the pecking order, so they drew special attention from the TAC Officers. They were not supposed to have their berets with them in flight school, but they had earned them the hard way, and were not going to give them up. It didn't take the TACs long to find the forbidden head gear. One morning we were standing in formation waiting to begin our exercises, when it was brought to our attention that a Green Beret hat had been nailed to a telephone pole, about twenty feet off ground.

The offending owner had to find a way to retrieve it, and once he did, he was told that since the beret was now dead, we had to perform a military funeral. The TACs told us that we were all going to Vietnam, and some of us would die. It only made sense to be able to learn how a military funeral was conducted. So a couple of days later we did a full burial according to the Army manual.

There was also another story going around at the time concerning a Green Beret, who was sneaking off base to visit Martha Rae. She had been to Vietnam several times to put on shows, and she had a real soft spot for the Special Forces. She had fallen in love or lust with one of them, and when he was accepted to flight school, she followed along. Martha took up residency in the Baker Hotel in Mineral Wells, and had her boyfriend over every chance she could. I don't know if Martha pulled strings with the brass or not. She was a Colonel in the Army Reserves, and a nurse, and knew a lot of people. Or maybe the boyfriend was just sneaking off base. That is what they were trained to do.

When we first started WOC training, we were assigned to a new building set up like a four story apartment complex. We had two students per room, and we had to maintain the area to meet the high expectations of the TACs. It wasn't too difficult because everything was fairly new. We had inspections weekly and sometimes daily. The TACs were always trying to catch us with unshined boots and shoes, or clothes that were not hung exactly one inch apart in the closet. Everything had to be perfect all of the time, or you racked up demerits. Enough of those, and you didn't go anywhere on the weekend.

Out of nowhere we were told to pack everything, as we were moving to a new building. We stuffed everything we owned in duffle bags, and then carried them about a mile to the old, two-story, wooden WWII buildings on the other side of Ft. Wolters. These hadn't been opened in years, and were full of dust and dirt. We had moved from a two men to a room palace, to a twenty men to a room dump. We were issued mattresses and bedding, and then picked out a bunk bed to call home. I was in a corner and grabbed the top bunk thinking, I would at least have some air up there.

This all took place on a Saturday and we were told we had to meet inspection standards by Monday. "Good God." This place hadn't seen a broom in years. We were given buckets and mops and a floor buffer, and told to hit it. By Monday the place was looking livable, but we failed the inspection, and were restricted again.

We quickly learned what to do and what not to do, in order to pass the inspections. Older soldiers taught us how to use certain waxes and polish on our shoes and boots to make them shine, and by using wax and the buffer we could get the floor to sparkle. The TACs were devious, and had a million ways to issue demerits. Just when you thought you knew all of their tricks, they would show you another. One climbed up on an upper bunk, and then turned his wrist so his watch was facing down. If he couldn't read it in the floor's reflection; demerits. Or they might lift your buck bed up a foot or so, and then drop it. A cloud of dust would fall out of the tubing. Who the hell thought of dusting the inside of a bed frame. More demerits were accrued. I remember one inspection, when I thought I had seen every trick the TACs could pull, and I was ready. My boots were shined beyond brilliant, and every item of clothing was folded, rolled or hung to perfection. You could bounce a quarter off my bed and get twenty-four cents in change. Every little piece of thread had been snipped from my uniform, so the inspector couldn't, "pull the lanyard and make me go boom." (A lanyard was the rope that was yanked to make a cannon go off.) I knew I was going home for the weekend.

I was standing there looking all spiffy and proud, when I heard the TAC Officer say to me, "Take off your belt, and remove your belt buckle." What the hell is this? I did as he said, and handed him my belt buckle, which had been buffed to a high gloss. I had even learned to my dismay in an earlier inspection, to not forget the back of the buckle. What could this shit head be looking for? The next thing I see is him prying the buckle apart, and then asking me, "Why isn't the inside shined Candidate Lazares?" Damn! Restricted again.

The TACs made you quake in your boots. I can hardly wait to get to Vietnam just to get away from these assholes. Better yet. I want to survive Nam, so I can come back and be a TAC, and wreak havoc on new WOCs.

# KILLER HILLER

After a month of pushups, sit-ups, inspections every time you turned around, classes all day and studying all night, we advanced to Flight Training. Now stuff got real interesting. And of course people really started to screw with us numb nuts. It wasn't unusual to see an instructor or TAC Officer pull someone to the side and start whispering in their ear. Then the candidate would take off running down to the heliport to find, "One hundred feet of flight line or a bucket of prop wash." Some of us had never been around aircraft or aircraft lingo and we were easy prey. Here you would be running hither and yon, until you finally found some mechanic standing around, and asked him where you could find the above items. Some would just call you a dumb ass, and others might explain that the area where the helicopters were parked was a flight line, and the wind put out by the rotors or propellers was prop wash. Having now learned this, the dumb ass couldn't wait to find someone newer than themselves to pull this trick on.

Ft. Wolters at this time had a main heliport and two additional heliports named Downing and Dempsey. Ft. Wolters started with about 125 OH-23s, and the number of helicopters was now over 1000, with the TH-55 now in the fleet. Scattered around the Texas desert were 7 stage fields, which all had western themed names such as, Pinto, Mustang, and Ramrod. These stage fields consisted of 4 lanes with 4 concrete pads in each lane.

When it was time to fly the main heliport was organized chaos. All these students and instructors heading for the main takeoff spots were hovering down lanes, and there might be fifty to 100 birds moving at a-time. Once they all got into the air they would either do maneuvers out over the desert, or they would head for the stage fields to work on take offs and landing. Depending on which lane you were assigned, you would land to the first pad open and then as aircraft departed, you would hover to the next pad and so on, until you were next for takeoff. All of this was controlled by a portable tower which directed the traffic. And just in case you screwed up there was a fire truck and a couple of fireman assigned to the stage field.

I was still learning everything I needed to be a Warrant Officer, and added to this was meteorology, aerodynamics, map reading, helicopter airframes and power plants, characteristics of flight, military history, chain of command for the entire army, and other stuff I can't even remember. These classes occurred for half of every day and the other half was now dedicated to learning to fly.

We were assigned to an instructor pilot (IP) and each IP had three students. Half the class was assigned to the H-23 Hiller (*if you can fly that piece of shit you can fly anything in the Army*) and the TH-55 (*the Mattel Messerschmitt*). I got the H-23 and a civilian instructor by the name of Dan Mock. This man had no sense of humor. I guess he had been scared too many times by new students. He carried a stick with him, and would beat you on the helmet with it if you displeased him. I remember one time he and I were flying along, and he yelled at me,

"Which way is the wind blowing Candidate Lazares?" Actually what he really said was, "Hey dumb shit. Do you have a clue what the hell you are doing?" He then shut the throttle. You always had to know the wind direction in case your helicopter quit, or the IP shut off the throttle to simulate an engine failure. You would always try to land into the wind. At this time in my life I was a fledgling smart ass. So I stuck my finger in my mouth and then out the open door, and then pointed straight ahead. Yup! Got hit on the head with the stick.

The standard was ten hours or less of dual training and you would solo. So each day the IP would take off with one student in the helicopter, while the other two rode a bus out to a stage field. A student and the IP would spend about an hour en-route, practicing all the things you would need to get safely off the ground and back again. This included hovering, auto rotations, landing in confined spaces and how to write a "Last Will and Testament" in case you screwed up.

As the day progressed each student would get his chance to terrify the instructor, while the other two would study or wander around the stage field trying to find an armadillo to harass. If you found one they would curl up in a defensive ball and pretend they were dead. So you would pick them up and toss them in the air, and if they were a smart armadillo they would pop open before they landed, and then run off and hide.

Finally, I managed to acquire enough skills that the IP allowed me to solo. I was never quite sure when this would occur, but I would be doing takeoffs and landings when all of the sudden, the IP would get out of the helicopter and tell me not to kill myself or ding the bird. Talk about a sweat storm. I had to hover up to the take off pad and then take off. I climbed out to 500 feet and made a right turn. I then made another quick right turn, and flew down wind until I got to the end of the stage field. Two more right turns had me lined back up with my lane, and I began a descent to the first open pad.

I repeated this four times while Mock stood there and watched. When I did the required loops around the traffic pattern I returned to the stage field and hovered over to Mr. Mock. He said, "Congratulation, you have managed to solo. Now, get out of my helicopter, so the other two idiots have a chance".

There was a quaint custom going on at the time which required the newly minted, solo pilot, to obtain a rock. Upon it, you paint your name, date of solo, and how many hours this all took. These were called "WOC Rocks" and I still have mine somewhere. Probably used as a door stop in the spare bathroom. Some classes picked up their rocks at the stage field or out in the desert, but not us. This was Texas and there were cattle ponds to use. So during the ride back to Ft. Wolters the bus would stop alongside a cattle pond, and your fellow aviators would drag you out, and throw you into the cattle pond. You then had to grope around and find a rock suitable for immortality. This was all accomplished after my solo, and cold wet and stinky I rode back to the barracks clutching my chunk of Texas.

# SNAKES

After I soloed, the IP would then spend more time with my other two stick buddies to get them ready. I would just ride out to the stage field in the bus, and spend the time studying. The day after I soloed this is how I was supposed to spend my day, but I was bored and decided to wander around. I headed off down the road and found myself back at the cattle pond which was maybe a ¼ mile from the stage field. I looked down and saw water moccasins swimming everywhere. I about died. I ran back to the stage field, and got a couple of the other students to come with me to verify what I saw. There were a large proportion of southern students in the army, and they confirmed that what I saw were in fact moccasins. Now this tended to put a real damper on throwing people into cattle ponds, so we solved this problem by stopping along the road back to base, and letting the new pilot find a rock. This was then taken to the post swimming pool and thrown in the deep end, along with the newly minted pilot. I always felt that this was the sissy way of doing things but I wish I could have done it this way, and avoided the lingering nightmares filled with snakes.

When we had all soloed we had our mandatory party at the post swimming pool, which included lots of beer and a barbeque. During the course of this little love fest one pilot would drown, and three people would get bit by a rattlesnake. I'll bet the new army just doesn't party like we used to.

Everyone was getting a little drunk because we had led such a sheltered existence to this point. We hadn't had anything to drink or been allowed to blow off stress and steam. It was dark out and most were hanging around the pool or the barbeque area when someone said, "Hey isn't that Kyle lying on the bottom of the pool. I wonder what he's doing.

"It looks like he drowned. Do you think we should pull him out?"

"No. Leave him. He's an asshole anyway."

Sober minds prevailed and a couple of guys jumped in and pulled him out. We were only a block from the base hospital, so several of us carried him to the emergency room. By this time he had revived and was spitting, choking, and generally puking up pool water on the rescuers, so he went from victim, back to being an asshole.

At the emergency room we found pandemonium. Near the swimming pool was a picnic area with a small stream running through it. It's a favorite place for those in the know to have a blanket and something to drink; someone to share it with, and maybe a little horizontal boogie. On this particular evening a sergeant and his lady were down by the creek, when she decided she needed to relieve herself. Not wanting to walk all the way to the pool area to use the restroom, she squatted down in the tall grass by the water. The next thing the sergeant knew is he heard a scream from his lady, and rushed to her rescue. She was standing there with her pants down and he inquired as to her problem. She said, "Something bit me. Here hold it."

She then handed a rattlesnake to the sergeant in case he has missed seeing it. At that point, the pissed off snake bit the sergeant. Being a trained military member, the sergeant thinks that it would be a good idea to take his lady, with the snake bit butt, the snake in question, and himself across the street to the emergency room. He knows in his mind that the hospital staff can more effectively treat them, if they have the snake for a positive identification.

As they arrived at the hospital, yelling and screaming for help, the night shift intern came out to find out what all the commotion was about. At this point the sergeant says, "She got bit in the ass by a snake, and I got bit in the hand by a snake, and here it is."
At which time he shoves the snake at the doctor who now also gets bit. We can't figure out why no one in the hospital wants to spend time with a drunk, waterlogged, almost drowned WOC pilot.

Now that we have soloed, we spend less and less time with the IP, and more on our own learning to become proficient at all the rudimentary aviator skills. We are also turned loose in west Texas doing cross country training. I would take off with a map and a destination, and maybe two or three check points and then the return flight. One of the common flight plans sent me from Ft. Wolters to Mineral Wells with a right turn. Then I flew north to Jacksboro, and made another right turn. The next leg would take me Southeast to Weatherford, and finally another right turn, and back home to the heliport.

There were basically three types of flight rules for cross country flying. One was VFR which meant, "Visual Flight Rules." That meant if you could see the sky and see the ground, both at the same time, you could go fly. The next type of flight rule was IFR. This stood for, "Instrument Flight Rules." This rule applied for those times you could not see your hand in front of your face, because clouds and stuff were in your way. You would have to fly using your radio and instrument gauges. The last flight rule was IFRR. This was the rule most new army aviators used. It was simple. You flew cross country and never got lost by the expedient means of, "I Follow Roads and Railroads." If in doubt to your location, drop down and take a look at the green sign on the side of the highway. Or find some railroad tracks and follow them to the next town. A Warrant Officer Aviator is never lost. He may be temporarily disorientated, but he is never lost.

It would be quite a sight watching maybe thirty or forty helicopters launching into the air, and then buzzing around because some can't seem to figure out west from east, or north from south. There would be copters all over sky with some down at ten feet above the desert trying to figure out a highway sign, and others going around and around a small town water tower, and trying to read the name. Another problem I encountered on these long two hour flights was thirst.

"*Praise the lord.*" There was an enterprising bar owner who had this huge parking lot with a windsock in the back lot. A windsock is used to tell you the direction of the wind. It wouldn't be too long into the cross country, when there would be four or five helicopters parked in the lot, while the intrepid aviators took on nourishment.

The end of each cross country trip would result in several helicopters coming back on lowboy trucks because they ran out of gas. If you keep flying in the wrong direction, for too long a time, you run low on gas. You just can't land at the local Texaco and pull up to the pumps. There were also the pilots who maybe hit a tree landing in an unauthorized place like a bar or a girlfriend's back yard.

The United States Army was also buying a lot of turkeys during the years that Fort Wolters, was hosting the flight school. All over that part of Texas, were turkey farms, and most were quite large. Fledgling aviators would buzz a farm to see what was in all the sheds, or more likely to find out if there was maybe a farmer's daughter, standing around waiting for her dream date. The stupid turkeys would stampede and kill themselves trying to escape the helicopter. The next day Uncle Sam would get a bill for a couple of hundred, "Butterballs."

I finally earned enough merits, or should I say, I finally quit earning demerits. I was allowed to start spending Friday night, through Sunday afternoon with Heleen, at our little house.

On one of these weekends we decided to get a bunch of us together and go on a picnic, so we stopped at the barracks to pick up a volley ball. I parked and ran into the barracks and found a friend named Barry, on his back snoring, with a baby skunk wrapped around his neck. Both of them were sound asleep. I shook Barry awake, and told him he had skunk in bed with him, and he said he knew that. I then asked if I could have the skunk, and Barry said sure, and handed the little critter to me. I ran outside to the car to show Heleen my new friend, and she started shaking her head and mouthing, "No. Hell No!" I took the skunk back inside and shook Barry awake again. I handed him the skunk and told him to keep him for me. I'd be back.

I found out later that Barry and some others had gone out drinking, and ended up at Lake Possum Kingdom. They were driving back and found the skunk walking down the road. Barry got out and grabbed it, and not wanting to get sprayed, they drove all the way back with the skunk hanging out the window. No wonder the skunk was tired.

The first thing on Monday morning, I had some free time, so I put the skunk in a box and drove to our house. Heleen wasn't home so I left the skunk and the box on the dining room table with a note, "Take care of my little friend and I will be back on Friday night." I didn't know what to expect when Friday rolled around. I was surprised to find "Ambrosia" and Heleen the best of friends, and playing all over the house. It took me two weeks to find some vet that would sanitize Ambrosia but we never had a problem with him spraying.

Shortly after we acquired the skunk, Heleen went to the animal shelter and came home with a small black baby dachshund. "Waldy" and Ambrosia became instant best friends and would wrestle and chase each other all over the house. And of course Ambrosia would get mad at Waldy, turn his back, lift his tail and then stamp his hind-legs to spray, but nothing would come out.

One of our little treats on the weekends, was to go to the local drive-in movie theatre. It was the only entertainment we could afford. We would load up the car with a cooler and some lawn chairs, and head on out. One evening we got in the car to see a movie, but saw all of this movement at the intersection. The whole street was moving. We pulled up and there was a swarm of locust moving through, which brought out the tarantulas. These babies were the size of a saucer and were jumping up and down to get the bugs. It was like a feeding frenzy. Some of those spiders were jumping as high as the window on the car. We finally quit watching and drove to the theatre.

Half the vehicles were pickup trucks and they would park backward. Everyone would sit in the bed of the truck and watch the movie. People in cars would sometimes yank the back seat out and then sit on that in the middle of the road. And others brought their lawn furniture, and set up in the aisles. It was like a neighborhood party. I don't remember anyone having a problem with anyone else. The kids would be down in front of the movie screen, playing on the swings and slide, and would usually stay there until the movie was over.

We were soon ready for graduation from Ft. Wolters and were scheduled to head for Ft. Rucker for instrument training, Huey helicopter transition, and the awarding of our wings and Warrant Officer Bars. But first we had to have a party.

# PIG PARTY

One of the traditions for the graduation party was to invite bus loads of young women from Denton Girls College. They were to be the dates for the single WOCs. These young maidens thought that they were coming to be danced and romanced by fledgling aviators, but in reality they were a means to an end. This was the largest pig party in Texas, and a lot of money was placed on who could date the ugliest girl. When the buses arrived the pilots would be standing there shoving beautiful women to the side so that they could get at the girl with the overbite, hairy arm pits, or the one with the wooden leg. There was about $300 riding on this, and we only made about $120 a month, so this was a substantial amount to those in the pool. There were about eight of us who were married, and would hold the money and judge the contest. So all night, these single guys would be parading their dates by our table to see who was going to win. I don't remember the details as the alcohol intake was substantial, but somebody walked off with the prize, and probably even married the girl.

Now it was time to pack up the car and head for Ft. Rucker, Alabama. Heleen was newly pregnant, and experiencing all the things that go with that condition. It was hotter than hell, and we had a car stuffed full of everything we own, plus the dog and the skunk. Our car was a 66' Dodge Charger, so the back seat folded down. The rear was crammed full of suitcases and boxes, and on top of all that is the skunk riding, in a bird cage. We would be driving along the freeway, and a car would pass, only to hit their brakes, and end up back next to us with everyone staring at the skunk. Sometimes we would pull off for gas, and a bunch of cars would follow so they could see the skunk up close.

The first night we stopped in San Antonio, TX at a motel. I went into the lobby and asked for a room, and inquired about the pet policy. I explained that I had a house-broken, small dachshund, and the guy said that's fine. I then told him I had a house broken skunk, and I thought he was going to have a cow. He finally relented, but told me we had to use the back stairs, and not let anyone else see the skunk. We got to our room and I gave Ambrosia and Waldy a bath in the tub. I no sooner got them out when there was a knock on the door. I figured it was manager coming to tell us he had changed his mind, but when I opened the door there stood some of the other guests. Word had spread, and they all wanted to see and pet the skunk. So now that the cat was out of the bag, so to speak, we loaded up the two of them and went down to the pool for a swim.

## ALABAMA AND MORE SNAKES

That remained the pattern on the drive from Texas to Alabama. We finally arrived in the southern part of Alabama. Of course, had to stop at some little gas station in the middle of nowhere, because Heleen had to pee again. It seemed like this was now occurring about every 15 minutes. She went off to find the facilities, and I was standing around the car, when this old Chevy pickup pulled in. Next thing I knew I have this crusty old farmer wearing his bib overalls and straw hat staring at me and my car. He said, "Hey boy. Think you have big snakes in Texas?" I told him I really wasn't from Texas, but that we bought the car there and it has Texas plates. He drug me over to his pickup, and there in the back is a rattlesnake that took up the entire bed of this truck. It was as big around as your forearm, and had twenty-two rattles on the tail. This old guy was pulling out of his farm and the snake was wrapped around his fence post, so he whacked it with a shovel and threw it in the back of the truck. It remained the biggest snake I ever seen, until a certain morning in Vietnam. You may notice a theme to my stories and it continues, which will explain my hatred (read fear) of snakes.

We arrived at Ft. Rucker and signed in to post. There was nowhere to live, as all post housing was taken by Warrant Officer instructors pilots, school cadre, and returning Vets. So off we went in search of a mansion, on a WOC's pay. We located a trailer in a little park not far from the post, and since it was fully furnished, we took it. Little did we know what we were in for? This park had dirt roads which caused everything to be coated in dust. The local farmers had hogs, which they let run through the trailers knocking over the garbage cans to get free eats. The local garbage men would go through your trash, and report you to the police if there were whiskey or beer bottles. This was a dry county and they took that very seriously, mainly because the fines were a real nice source of income. To make the situation a little more bizarre, Heleen took to doing walks around the trailer court with the dog and skunk following her. The two animals would chase each other, and roll around in the dirt, then the skunk would start with the feet stamping again.

I had two buddies who were living on base, but they were not allowed to keep their motorcycles there, so we kept them at our trailer. One was a nice Triumph and the other was a Matchless 650. They would come out and ride them when they could, and I was free to borrow them whenever I wanted. Sometimes on the weekends, I would put Heleen on the back of the bike, stuff the skunk in my coat pocket, and Heleen would carry the dog. By this time Heleen was really starting to show her new baby bump. Off we would go to tour the area or have lunch in a bar. "Hi. Set 'em up for me and my friends".
I got some real strange looks when I set Ambrosia on the bar top, and it made for a real conversation piece wherever we went.

The little old lady that owned the trailer park was a southern belle, and a true Alabamian. She was in the town of Enterprise shopping at the Piggly Wiggly, when she was body checked into the frozen foods by a black lady. Well our dear sweet little old landlord did what any self respecting lady of the South was expected to do, and stabbed the other lady a couple of times, with her old folding pen knife. The police showed up and took her to jail for the remainder of the day so she could cool off, and then gave her a ride back home.

That was Alabama justice in 1966.

Now we began the phase of flight training that I just hated, instruments. They had the OH-13 for this portion of flight school. The -13 had a large bubble front end, which was called the fish bowl, and seats for two. For instrument training they would paint the student's part of the bubble white. Then they would mount this hood over your helmet, so that you could only look straight ahead at the panel gauges. Talk about claustrophobic. You could not see a thing, and yet were expected to bore holes in the sky and get from point A to B, and maybe back again, using nothing but instruments.

To illustrate how this works, picture being in your car, and someone has painted all the windows so you can't see out. On the dash you have a compass and of course your speedometer. Now a little voice tells you to drive and they will tell you when to speed up, slow down, brake and turn. Your life is in the hands of the voice and you hope it doesn't steer you into a wall or another car. This was some *scary shit* and was not designed to make you proficient. It was only to maybe get you out of trouble, should you find yourself in the clouds, surrounded by mountains, in Vietnam. Which is exactly what happened more than once.

If you were having difficulties with this portion of flying, they would arrange for you to spend time in the "flight simulator" or as we called it, "The Box". The simulator was about the size of the carton your refrigerator came in. It contained the same instruments as your helicopter including the collective (stick that makes the helicopter go up and down) and the cyclic (which makes the helicopter turn, climb or descend). It also had rudder pedals (which kept the nose straight or helped you turn). To fly a helicopter you had both hands going at all times, plus you were twisting the throttle on the collective to increase or decrease power. Now throw in the feet, which were always pushing on one or the other pedals, and your head which never quits moving. Add eyes, that always have to scan the instruments. Helicopters have a tendency to have something break, fall off, or quit, and the instruments are your first indicator that you may want to land somewhere.

On top of all this we now have the little voice on the radio telling us that even though we can't see, we are going to climb, descend, turn, and land, all while being stuffed in this box with no visual reference to the real world. Oh! Did I mention that this flight simulator is able to rock, roll, pivot, spin and generally make you airsick the whole time. The CIA has really screwed up with all the water boarding. They just needed to buy up the old flight simulators, and strap the terrorist in for a ride. They would spill their guts in more ways than one.

I earned a couple of warnings and a pink slip and had to retake the instrument check ride, but I eventually passed and moved on to the Huey. I may not have made it clear, but in the beginning and all through WOC training and flight school, if for any reason you were unable to meet the standards, and pass each and every phase, you were gone. The army would then send you to cook and bakers school, or make you a ground pounder, so you could walk around Vietnam.

I finally passed the instrument phase and was now advanced to the work horse of the Vietnam War, the Huey. The Huey just basically flew itself, and the pilot was along to look at all the cool scenery, and pose in his tailored flight suit. Everything I had flown up to this point was little, two-man helicopters. I was now the pilot of this monster that can hold a crew of four, and maybe six to eight combat troops. I was going to be learning the meat and potatoes of Vietnam, combat flying. I was taught low level, cross county navigation, formation flights to and into landing zones, and simulated combat assaults both day and night.

Formation flying is real stressful until it soon becomes second nature. The first couple of times the instructor is continually telling you to close in on the aircraft next to you. It's not long he's telling you that you might want to back off a little. *I'll show him who has the cajones.*

Then there is my very favorite part of flying the Huey, gunnery. I got to spend a couple of days flying on the gunnery range, firing machine guns, that were fixed, on the sides of the helicopter. That memory still gives me a wet spot in my pants, but if I stick a towel in my shorts, no one will notice.

# END OF THE EASY LIFE

Near the end of school I got to participate in a little exercise called E and E. This referred to the escape and evasion course set up in the swamps and woods of southern Alabama. This of course is the same Alabama that has water moccasins, rattlesnakes and giant man eating gators. I had to get from point A to B at night without getting caught by the enemy troops. These were Green Berets and other like minded individuals who were selected to be the "enemy" based on their desire to screw with us new pilots.

I was put with a team of six other students and provided with one live chicken which we were to kill, clean and eat. I just couldn't imagine myself doing this after the trauma I experienced as a young man in the chicken factory. I had Heleen cook a couple of chicken breasts and wrap them tight. I hid them in my pants and when the rest of the team was figuring a way to kill our chicken, I had dinner.

My team got dropped off in the forest about 4:00 PM and we had to get ready for the E & E exercise before it got dark. Once it got dark we were to head south and not get captured.

Meanwhile the "enemy" secreted themselves all along the various roads we had to cross. They were armed with flare guns and if they heard you they would fire flares at head height to get you to lie down and then they would capture up the unlucky evaders. It took me all of five minutes to realize that six guys made a whole lot more noise than two guys. I and another intrepid soul waved bye bye to the group and away we went. I don't remember how far we had to travel but the objective was a village with a landing zone nearby. If you didn't get caught and made it to the LZ, then a helicopter would come in and rescue you. If you were captured then a different fate awaited you.

The classmates who got captured were taken to the village and placed in a large hut together. Here they were humiliated, tortured a little and interrogated. Nothing real physical was done to them as the U.S Army had a lot of money invested in us, plus we were going to Vietnam soon to be shot at for real. Toward morning everyone in the hut was told that there was a secret trapdoor in the floor that led to a tunnel, and that they could crawl through the tunnel, get outside the fence and then make their way to the LZ to hitch a ride home. What they failed to mention was that in the spirit of adventure the Green Berets had built a cage out of chicken wire and placed it in the side of the tunnel and in the cage was a pissed off rattlesnake.

Now these poor guys were crawling along in the dark trying to escape when they start hearing screaming from the front of the line and the word: "SNAKE!" No one can turn around and they can't back up and several aviators are pissing their pants, but hey fun is fun.

# DRESS BLUES, TENNIS SHOES, AND A LIGHT COAT OF OIL

Finally it was graduation day. I got sworn in as brand new baby Warrant Officer-1, and then Heleen got to do the honors of pinning on my Aviator Wings. As we left the auditorium where the ceremony was held, the enlisted staff for the flight class was all lined up to salute us. As tradition dictates, we hand them a new silver dollar for being the first to recognize us as officers. Except for a few old guys, this group is made up of kids nineteen to twenty years old, who after thirty days leave, get to head for the war.

We were all waiting for orders to see where we would end up, and I remember telling Heleen that she shouldn't worry, because as long as I didn't get the 1st Cav. I should be fine. At that time everyone was talking about the Cav. They were in more shoot 'em ups than anyone, and lived and breathed helicopter assaults. So can you guess where I got orders to? They can kill me, but at least they can't eat me. I think that is against the law.

The last official act was the graduation dinner dance. We all got prettied up in our Dress Blue uniforms with our new wings and WO 1 insignia. Heleen and the other wives had their hair done, and were wearing new dresses. Heleen was five months pregnant, and had this radiant Madonna look going on. All the wives looked beautiful but they all seemed to have this strange look in their eyes. They had been through hell with their boy aviators the past year, and now we're going to face brand new challenges and terrors. It was very bitter sweet as we had all been together for almost a year, and were now scattering to all points of the compass. The wives would be left behind, but some of us would see each other again in Vietnam.

Heleen and I packed the car for the drive back to Washington. We loaded up the dog, and kissed the skunk goodbye. We had some trailer park friends who graduated with us, and would be going back to their farm in the Midwest. Ambrosia had a home with them. I don't remember the exact figures, but this fellow pilot had like four girls, not including the wife. With that many women in one household it was no wonder he wanted to go to Vietnam.

Heleen was going to be staying with her parents while I was gone, and while she waited to give birth to our first child. I could not tell you a single thing about the trip home, or the remaining thirty days leave I spent with Heleen, in Washington. Seems like we got in the car and the next thing I remember, is getting on a plane to fly to Vietnam.

# 2/20 ARA

HUEY WITH 48 ROCKETS

# HOG

I flew out of Travis AFB, in California on a C 141. There is nothing like spending twenty-three hours flying backward, in a cold drafty noisy airplane. We were handed box lunches, which contained a sandwich, chips and a cookie. This would be our meal on the flight, and would be repeated two more times. The plane was loaded with soldiers heading to the 1st Cav. as replacements. Everywhere I looked were enlisted men, and I can't recall seeing anyone I knew. There may have been other officers, and maybe even some WO pilots but with 150 people pressed in there, it was hard to tell. I was invited up on the flight deck with the Air Force pilots. They took pity on me, and let me catch a nap in their crew rest area.

We stopped for fuel in Guam and as we were landing everyone was told to stay away from the windows, and not take pictures. The B-52s that were bombing North Vietnam were stationed there, and of course everyone in the world knew this, but for some reason all the U.S. military men on this airplane had to pretend that the airplanes weren't there.

We arrived over Pleiku, South Vietnam and began a very tight spiral down to the airfield. This was to avoid the embarrassment of having the 141 shot down by some rice farmer with a WWII rifle. Pleiku was located in the central highlands, and at this time was the place where a lot of the major battles were taking place. I was to spend the night here and then hitch a ride the next day to An Khe, home of the 1st Cav. Pleiku was near the western border with Laos and Cambodia, and An Khe was east of there. Both places were located on plateaus in the mountain ranges, and as you continued east you dropped down to the coastal plain and the South China Sea. I had something to eat and a drink in some club, and then made my way to a bunk I had been assigned to.

The daytime temperature was somewhere around 110 degrees, and then at nighttime, it would drop down into the 70's. With a forty degree difference from the day to the night, it would feel very cold. I was bundled up in my flight suit and a sweater, and was stuffed into my mummy sleeping bag, with nothing showing but my face. During the night I woke up because something heavy was sitting on my chest. I looked down and this huge rat was staring at me. I figured out that I needed to overcome this threat, so after some careful thought, I screamed like a little girl, while throwing my hands and arms straight up from inside the sleeping bag. This in turn, launched the rat toward the next person down the line. I immediately rolled over and got all exposed skin face down on the bunk. I stayed that way all night, too afraid to go back to sleep.

The next day we flew down to An Khe. At the headquarters for the 1st Cav. all of us new pilots were packed into a tent, and this is where we would be assigned to all the various aviation units. This Lt. Colonel asked if any of us knew which unit we wanted to be assigned to, and I put up my hand, and asked for the 2/20 Ariel Rocket Artillery . In flight school I had met a former Cav. pilot who told me that I should try and get into the ARA. He said that they get to fire rockets all of the time, but from a nice safe altitude, and it's a better than being a bus driver. Anyone flying the Hueys in the lift companies and flying soldiers from here to there was referred to as a, "slick pilot" or the more derogatory, "bus driver".

I was told to stand to the side with some other pilots who had selected their units. This Lt. Colonel asked of those left, who was married. When some hands went up he sent them to stand with my group. He next asked who had dependents, or was an only child. They also joined us. He then informed those remaining that they would be assigned to the 1/9th Cav. which was primarily a scout unit with gunships and grunts assigned. They would be out looking for the enemy, and if they found them they would attack. They were always in firefights, and a lot of helicopters were being shot up. The life expectancy of a young scout pilot was judged to be about two weeks. You would either be dead or wounded within that time frame, so they didn't want old guys, married guys, or guys with dependants. They wanted nineteen and twenty year olds who thought they were invincible, or were just too dumb to know they could get killed.

A Private had been sent to pick me and my duffel bag up, and I was driven over to my new home. There I was assigned to one of the gun platoons, and shown to my hooch. This was a hut built on stilts with bamboo walls and a thatched roof. It looked like something out of the movie, "South Pacific". There was even a banana tree next to the front porch and you could pick a snack off of it whenever you wanted. At that time there were a few warrant officers living in this hooch. The captains and lieutenants had their own building.

Inside were one and two man rooms with bamboo dividers between them. I was given a small, one-man room that had nothing in it except for an army cot and a foot locker. A couple of pilots living in the last room, had a trap door in the floor with a set of steps that went down to an underground bunker. The bunker was lined with wood scrounged from ammo boxes, and they had used a blow torch to burn the wood, and make it look like expensive paneling. The two of them used this for their shelter if we got hit or over run, but it was really their music center. They had a reel to reel tape player and stereo system plus a couple of guitars.

I was sent down to the supply room to gather all the stuff I would need to exist in my new environment. I drew a new helmet, chicken plate (*this isn't a dish in a restaurant*) .38 cal. revolver, bedding and assorted other items. A chicken plate was a vest like contraption that went over your head, and was secured with Velcro on the sides. The front and back had pockets about the size of a book, and in these were armored plates designed to stop bullets. They would stop most small caliber rounds if fired from a great distance, but nothing large or close. Besides if you are wearing body armor, they would probably miss the armored plate anyway.

The supply sergeant then told me I needed a body bag. I didn't want to know why. He laughed, and said he pulled that joke on all the new guys. We later refined this little gag and would send the new pilots down to supply for their body bag. The sergeant would tell them he was all out, but would then hand them a pile of sand bags. He would go on to explain that they had to cut the sacks open and lay them out. Then they had to be sewn together to form a bag. Lastly the new guy was to sew his name tag to it and carry the body bag everywhere he went. Man, was that funny, or at least we thought so.

Once settled, I found out I was the youngest pilot and also the newest. As such I was treated like a leper. No one knows how you will do as a pilot, or how you will react in combat, so they don't want to get too close to you. Or you just might get killed. I started fixing up my room in the hooch and started my orientation as a newbie. It was a lot to learn in a short time. I had to know all the names of the units we were supporting, and where they were located, plus their radio call signs. You also had to know the frequencies on the radio for all supporting units such as, artillery, medevac, the Air Force, all the different fire bases, ground units that were out in the jungle walking around, Green Berets, long range recon units, plus the Korean and Vietnam army. We had little books that contained all the information, but it was coded. You had to be able to figure out who you wanted to talk to and where in the book they were. Then you had to encode the information, figure out what you wanted to talk about, and then contact them. Sometimes you were going balls to the wall because they needed help right away, but you didn't dare screw up. You could end up shooting rockets at the wrong target.

I was now assigned to a platoon, 2/20 ARA. The parent unit was the 2/20 ARA Battery and it consisted of three platoons: A, B, and C. Each platoon consisted of twelve gunships. 90 % of all missions assigned to ARA were for calls of a fire mission, from a friendly unit in contact with the enemy.

ARA was essentially artillery fire, in support of troops using a helicopter platform. When the infantry needed to air assault into a landing zone, the fixed guns of the artillery would fire at that particular piece of real estate. This artillery fire had to stop one minute prior to the troop helicopters coming in to land. This provided the enemy with time to recover and prepare for the arrival of the infantry. So ARA was developed to fill that void. They would precede the lift ships and fire rockets into the landing zone, right up to the time the infantry was getting ready to land.

We were flying Huey B and C models which were the gunships. My aircraft had two rocket pods, which each carried twenty-four rockets, and was referred to as a HOG. Normally we would also have a crew chief and a door gunner, who were armed with M-60 machine guns. They were connected to the helicopter by a strap, and the M-60 hung from a bungee cord. That way they could cover the area in front, behind and underneath the chopper, and it did make for some interesting flying.

The bungee cords were later done away with because of the dangers and they went to a fixed mount for the M-60. It had stops so that the gun could only travel so far up and down. Or front to rear. You were hearing stories about some crew chief or gunner who got excited, and ended up shooting the front of the helicopter, or the tail boom, or putting holes in the rotor blades. There were even stories about some pilots being shot by their crew. A crew member might get shot and pull the trigger while going down, and spray the inside of the cockpit. With these stories going around the crew chiefs would love to get a new pilot and break them in. The crew would turn their M-60 sideways, and when they fired, direct the hot shell casings down the neck of the new pilot. The pilot would then start screaming that he had been shot, and he would try to climb out the window of the helicopter while doing 100 knots at an altitude of 1500 feet. I know I did. The crew chiefs and gunners found this hilarious.

A typical day at An Khe would usually consist of being on standby with another gunship, and having to respond to a call for help by getting airborne within two minutes. I would crank up the helicopter while the section leader would be getting the briefing on who, what, where, and why. "When" didn't matter because it was always now. He would run down, jump in and off we would go.

We would fly to where we were needed, and if the unit was in contact with the enemy, we would be directed to fire rockets. We normally would roll in from 1500 feet and shoot pairs of rockets at the target. As we got near we would break off our run, and then the door gunners would open up to cover our turns. We may do this once or we may keep coming in until all the rockets were expended, at which time we would be relieved by another pair of gunships. We would return to the air field to rearm and refuel. When we got back to the landing pad we would shut down the bird, and everyone would pitch in putting rockets together, and loading them into the rocket pods. The rockets were in two parts. A long rocket motor weighing twenty pounds, and a six pound war head that had to be screwed on to the motor.

The rockets were from WW II and had been used by the Air Force and Navy fighters as an air to air rocket for shooting down bombers. These were unstable and not effective, so were developed further for air to ground use during Korea. They were a 2.75" folding fin rocket with a war head and a four foot body. The stuff that made them whoosh through the air was part bat shit that was mined on some island, somewhere. These things were old and not always reliable. If they had been dropped, the propellant would crack and the rocket would misfire, or the electrical charge might not make contact. I just never knew what I was in store for. When I pushed the little red button on my cyclic that were supposed to send two rockets racing toward the enemy, sometimes one would fire and one would not. Or neither would fire, or a rocket would take off toward the ground, only to start climbing and looping, and maybe coming back toward me. There were also times that I pushed the red button for a pair, and had all 48 rockets cook off at the same time, which could make for some real interesting aerial maneuvers.

We usually landed on runways that were covered in PSP (pierced steel planking) and of course if you were coming in heavy, you had to slide onto the runway, because the Huey just wouldn't hover. This caused friction, which led to an electrical charge, which sometimes would cook off the rockets. This would truly scare the shit out of everyone. You think you are safe on friendly ground, when a helicopter lands, and a pair of rockets go whooshing down the runway.

We even had one event where the crew chief got out of the helicopter and walked up to open the pilot's door. A rocket cooked off and went right through him and the door, killing both. The normal procedure was for the crew to come forward from their seats near the guns, and open the two pilot's doors, then slide the armor plating back. This was a part of the armored seats and hopefully blocked bullets from coming in the side windows. After doing this they waited for the blades to stop turning, and then strapped them down. The crew chief would then ground the rocket pods so nothing external, like static electricity, could cause a rocket to fire. Who knows what cause that rocket to fire, but after that the grounding stakes went in first.

One of the fun things we did with the rockets was when we were on mortar patrol flying around An Khe at night. I would draw this duty every couple of nights, and it required flying around and around the perimeter of the base. The reasoning was, that if the base got hit then I could respond immediately to the sight of the intrusion, or to where the incoming enemy fire was coming from. I would then hit the spot with rockets and hold off the attack until the artillery could get into the act. To keep the enemy on guard, I would also randomly fire rockets at known positions during the night. This was known as H & I (harassment & interdiction) fire. These rockets when they come out of the pods, got to moving pretty good, and sort of crack the sound barrier. If you are right under them they can scare the "*Be-Jesus*" out of you. So part of our payback to all those who were asleep safe in their bunks, would be to come in low level over the hooches, and fire out toward the jungle. We especially liked to do this over the area where all the new arrivals would be spending their first nights. One pair of rockets would send them all running for the bunkers, as if the *"Hounds of Hades"* were on their ass. I did not think it was funny the first time I heard them fired over my head, but it sure became a riot later, when I was doing the shooting.

An Khe was located on a plateau. To our east was An Khe pass that went down to the flats, that ran to the South China Sea. To our west was another pass that climbed to another plateau where Pleiku was located. This pass was called Mang Yang, and it was here that the French Foreign Legion was ambushed back in 1954. Over 2,000 Legionnaires started an evacuation from An Khe, toward Pleiku and during five days of fighting, lost over half of their men. When you flew west up the pass you could still see the grave markers that had been erected, and along the road were the rusted hulks of their trucks and armored cars. This really puts history in perspective. I was too young to appreciate the fact that if the French couldn't defeat this primitive V.C, what chance did I have.

# SIN CITY

A short time after my arrival at An Khe we all piled in the unit truck, and headed down town, to pick up some of the necessities of life. I had to have a plastic pail to wash in and shave. And I had to have my own personal webbed, lawn chair. Once in a while we would have a movie, and you just couldn't sit in the dirt like a common soldier.

Another reason for the trip to town was that we could visit Sin City. This was a large, walled compound guarded by M.Ps. Inside were tailor shops, markets with souvenirs and lawn chairs, bars and of course bar girls. For a few dollars a G.I. could fall in love for an hour, and meet all of his basic needs. The 1st Cavalry's way of thinking was, that they would rather control what was going to happen, anyway. By sending the doctors down to Sin City, they ensured having the girls checked on a regular basis. Plus, no weapons were allowed and the M.Ps were there to keep order. All the prices were fixed, and no one was getting ripped off. I don't know when this started, but it was probably the day after the first American arrived. I know it ended when some seventeen year old G.I. wrote a letter home to mom and said: "You will never believe what the 1st Cav. has for me?" She immediately wrote her congressman, and that brought an end to Sin City. It also made a feature article in Life Magazine.

All of us new warrant officers were on the bottom of the list for perks. If there was a show of some kind at the officers club, you could bet that we would get to be Officer of the Day, while the lieutenants and captains got to see the show. It pissed us off, and so we came up with a plan to extract revenge. To facilitate pissing, the Corp. of Engineers would pound a large shell container into the ground, and then cover it with a metal screen. This way the urine was sent underground to leach back into the soil, as opposed to everyone just peeing on the ground, wherever they happened to be standing.

The U.S Army was not that far removed from the Stone Age and was still using what is called a field telephone. This consisted of two or more phones connected by black electrical wire, and to use the phone you cranked a handle. This sent an electrical charge down the wires. The phone on the other end would ring and then you could talk. It was like two tin cans with a string, only there was electricity involved. I took the bare, black wires and hooked them to the piss tube, and had the other ends connected to a field phone. I hid in the bushes outside the officers club, and it was only a question of time before some drunken officer would step out into the dark to use the facilities. Crank-Crank-Crank. On a dark night you could see the little bolt of lightning leap from the urinal to the penis, followed by a squeal of pain, and a few seconds of him dancing the Boogaloo or the Funky Chicken.

These field telephones were reminiscent of the phones in long ago America. In those days you picked up the earphone, and cranked on the handle until the operator answered. She then would crank on her end, to the phone you wanted to be connected to. Of course, there was no such thing as a private conversation. If you heard the ringing, you were free to pick up your phone and listen in, or interrupt and put your two cents worth in. Same with the field telephones.

Ring-Ring-Ring.

"Hello. Who is this?"

"Who do you want?"

"I need to speak to Major so and so."

"Well! This ain't him. Now get off the phone because I need to use it."

"Well! This is Colonel Whatever, and I want you off this phone."

"Well you can just kiss my ass Colonel."

"Who is this?"

"You don't know?"

"No. I don't"

"Perfect. Good bye."

If you were bored, you could spend an entire afternoon screwing with the brass.

We also had more modern facilities, than plain old piss tubes. These consisted of a wooden out house, with a plank bench, and holes cut out of the top of the plank to accommodate your average ass. Under the plank were fifty-five gallon barrels, that had been cut in half and filled with diesel fuel.

At the end of each day, the soldiers on shit detail would open the trap doors in back, and drag out the barrels. They would then light them on fire, and stand there and stir this concoction, until all was consumed.

Those on the permanent screw up list, would be assigned to be shit burners, and that is all they did each and every day. You could smell them a long way off, and they were always kept by themselves and down wind. These men had a sticky, sooty, greasy look to themselves, and their clothes. Every single day you would see them sitting by themselves, and they always looked the same. I am not sure you could ever get them, or their uniforms clean.

*"What did you do in the war daddy?"*

*"I can't talk about it. It's all classified top secret, but it did involve a stirring stick."*

I do not care where you might be standing, it seemed like the smoke was always in your face. There is no smell like it anywhere on earth, and it defies description, but if you smelled it once, you would never forget it. Someone could light off a shit barrel today, and I would instantly know what it is.

One morning after breakfast I was feeling the urge, and so headed down to the shitter, to contemplate life. I remember sitting there, with my elbows on my knees and my head in my hands, and just thinking about nothing in particular. All of a sudden my dog tag chain broke, and the whole thing dropped into the hole between my legs. I knew I was not going fishing for them, and figured I could just put in for a new set. The next morning, I was sitting in my hooch when there was a knock on the door. I asked who was there and this apparition appears, and asked for "Mr. Lazares." He stood there holding a set of dog tags, and wanted to know if I had lost them. He said he found them when he was burning the shit barrel and so he fished them out, and cleaned them up, and here they were.

"Oh! That Mr. Lazares. He went on a mission, and never came back. Just set them on the floor and I'll see his next of kin gets them."

# BON SON

I was in An Khe less than a month, when we received word that our unit was moving to the field. This would be the last time I lived, or slept in a building. It would be tents or the helicopter, for the next eleven months. We were heading for a former Green Beret camp called LZ Two Bits, which was near the town of Bon Son, not far from the South China Sea. When we arrived, the first thing we did was start filling sand bags, to build revetments to protect the helicopters. With the 1st Cav. the helicopters were the most important asset. They cost the most and were harder to acquire, and they were the reason for the Cav's, being in existence. It was much easier to replace a WO-1 Aviator. Over the course of the first few days, we filled sand bags, put up tents to live in, and of course flew missions day and night.

The war never stopped and neither did we. One day I was working on the tent, and trying to make my little space homier. We used ammo boxes for everything, and people became quite ingenious at building book cases, clothes closets, beds, and desks out of the boxes the rockets came in. I heard a commotion outside and a bunch of guys cheering and yelling. When I went out to look, there was some G.I. down below the hill, in the concertina wire. He had his air mattress laid out, and was buck naked, with some girl from the village. He finished, stood up and took a bow, and was immediately captured by his sergeant. I guess he should have been a little more discrete.

One evening around dusk we went outside our tent, which was set up on the top of a hill. Down below us was concertina wire, and beyond that rocks, trees and then a village. We had a soldier, in a little bunker guarding our area, and he had a starlight scope on his rifle. The starlight scope used whatever available light there was, and intensified it so that you could see at night. It turned everything green, but you could you see stuff that was invisible to the naked eye. Our guard said he saw a man crawl out of the bushes, and get down behind some rocks, that were at the base of the hill. He then called in to the Sgt. of the Guard and asked for permission to shoot. He got approval and told us what he was going to be doing. We all went into our tent and got our own M-16s.

There was about four or five of us, and we all opened fire on the rock pile. This kept up for about five minutes as we all sprayed rounds into the rocks, where the guard said he saw the man crawl. Nothing happened and we all got bored, so it was off to bed. The next morning we watched as some villagers came out, and went into the rocks. A couple of minutes later they came out carrying a dead body, and walked off to the village. That was the last we ever heard about the incident, and had no idea who he was, or what he was doing down there. He was probably just looking for a spot to screw off, so he wouldn't have to work.

Two Bits had been a Green Beret camp, so the area surrounding our camp was mined. No one knew where the mines were, so the commander called for some experts to locate the mines, and either move them or disarm them. We were sitting out on the sand bagged wall surrounding our tent, watching two guys on their hands and knees poking, and prodding down in the mine field. One of the guys hit a mine, which lifted him up in the air and over backward, where he then hit another mine.

He was bloody and not moving. The guy with him now started screaming, and everyone was yelling at him not to move, that we would get him out. Instead, he jumped up and started to run, but didn't get far, before he stepped on a mine and blew his foot off. He was lying there about ten feet from his partner, and screaming and crying. Another pilot and I ran up to a helicopter and pulled the rocket pods off. We started up, and hovered over the injured guy, so that the crew chiefs could pull him into the back. We then flew him up to LZ English, which was a major base about twenty miles north of Two Bits. He was dropped off at the medevac unit and we flew back to our home, so the crew chief could hose out the back of the helicopter. While we were gone, a couple of brave soldiers went into the mine field, and pulled out the body of the other guy.

We got called in one day for our mission briefing, and were told that we would also be carrying a crew from NBC or CBS. Our ship would have a cameraman and a reporter, and the other ship would have a sound man and a technician. After taking off, we headed for an area we were going to hit with rockets. This was to be a choreographed mission. The area was a free fire zone, and consisted of nothing of importance except trees. It was all for the benefit of the people back home in the U.S.A. They would get to see on the evening news, a brave helicopter crew, engaging the enemy.

I was flying when my controls started freezing up. I could barely push the collective up or down, and the cyclic has become a non-responsive stick. We had lost the hydraulics on the helicopter. It was the same sensation you experience loosing the power steering, and brakes in a car. It takes everything, to muscle the helicopter into doing what you need to get back on the ground. My co-pilot put out a mayday call advising our sister ship what was going on, and requesting help.

I ended up having to make an emergency landing in a rice paddy in the middle of nowhere. Luckily, we were over flat terrain with lots of rice paddies. The only bad part was the dikes that crisscrossed the area. Each rice paddy was a large square, bordered by the dikes that were a couple of feet tall, and used to control irrigation. The other pilot was now on the controls with me, to help get the helicopter down. I was bleeding off forward airspeed, and had lined up with a nice muddy field. The skids touched down and we started sliding across the goop, toward the dyke at the north end. The bird finally came to a rest, and we bailed out of the helicopter, and took up defensive positions while waiting to be rescued.

Our wingman was flying circles around the rice paddy at a couple of hundred feet, to scare off anyone with bad intentions. They informed us that a ready reaction force of soldiers was on the way, and they arrived shortly to set up a perimeter around us. Before they arrived I was lying there behind a little dike armed with a .38 pistol and six bullets, knowing at any time a hoard of enemy were going to come charging out of the trees. I looked up and in front of me are the camera man and his reporter, filming us and the helicopter.

A week later, I received a letter from home that said after this incident the story was shown in the U.S on the nightly news. At my family home someone told Heleen, "Hey. Isn't that Michael laying there in that rice paddy?"

The lesson learned from that little crash landing was, I could never carry enough stuff with me when I might find myself on the ground, preparing to repel invaders. After that day I always carried my .38 with a bunch of extra rounds, a K-bar knife that my father had carried in WWII, a .22 automatic with an extra clip, and a CAR 15, which is a shortened version of the M-16 and a whole lot of bullets in a bandolier. I was a walking arsenal, and could barely waddle to the helicopter with all the stuff I was carrying.

Life as a pilot in the 1st Cav. was nothing like what others experienced. I talked to friends who were flying Monday through Friday only, and never at night. They had a nice room with air conditioning, running hot and cold water, television, officer clubs with shows each weekend, and a dining hall with good, if not great food. Meanwhile, except for the first month at An Khe, I was living mostly in a tent, and I continued to live like this for the entire year. We were always moving somewhere, and so a lot of the time I slept either on the ground, or in the helicopter. My best friends were the air mattress and poncho liner that went everywhere with me. If we were on two minute standby, I would strap myself into my seat, and sleep sitting up. All I had to do was push the starter button, put my helmet on, and we were gone to shoot up trees and monkeys.

Every day a different pair of gunships was assigned as the two minute standby. If someone was in trouble, you were expected to launch within the two minutes, and be on your way to help. This was 24 hour duty, and if you responded to a call, another crew then became the standby ships. The aircraft commander (A/C) usually slept in the Operations Center, and would be briefed on the mission. They would send a runner down to the flight line to get the crew alerted. To save time, the crew chief and pilot would sleep in the aircraft. The crew chief would take the grounding wire off the rockets and release the rotor blades, while the pilot would start the engine. By that time the A/C would jump into his seat with the, who, what, and where information, and off we would go.

One night I was on the standby crew, and sleeping strapped into the right seat of the helicopter. The door gunner came running up and said we had a mission, so I cranked up and waited for the A/C and the other ship to get ready. We launched and headed for the An Loa Valley. It was about 2:00 a.m. and pitch dark. We were vectored into the area of extremely high mountains, just north of the valley floor, and met up with a Huey command and control helicopter. The C & C bird was controlling a Bird Dog spotter plane, which was flying blacked out just above the tree tops.

It was relayed to us that a Long Range Reconnaissance Patrol (LRRP) had been following an NVA Battalion for several days. When the LRRPs bedded down for the night in some thick bushes, they thought the battalion was also bedding down some distance away. Instead the NVA stopped, then restarted and moved to another location, and when they stopped for the night, the LRRPs were right in the middle of the enemy encampment.

The LRRP unit consisted of four men and they traveled light. They only carried a few rations, and a lot of ammo. Now they were surrounded by several hundred NVA, and were in danger of being found. The LRRP on the radio was whispering, and I could hear the fear in his voice. The NVA knew the Bird Dog was flying over them, but they were not going to shoot at it and give away their position. The Bird Dogs directed artillery, and would also vector in jets to bomb and strafe. The last thing any enemy unit wanted to do was bring all that destruction down itself.

A plan was finally worked out where Bird Dog would fly back and forth until directly over the LRRP unit. The Huey C&C bird would be right behind the Bird Dog, and when the LRRPs yelled now, the Huey would drop straight down and pick them up. Everything at that time, would get very hairy. That's where our two gunships came in. As soon as the pickup was made we were to roll in, and dump every rocket we had.

Everything was lined up, and the pickup was a go. The blacked out Bird Dog and the Huey started across the mountain top when the LRRPs began yelling, "Now!" The Huey dropped straight down, and the soldiers sprinted from their hiding place and clamored aboard. As soon as the C&C ship started back into the air, the entire mountain top erupted in enemy tracer rounds. I had never seen so much gun fire from one spot. I rolled in right under the C&C ship, and hit the mountain top with every rocket I had. My wingman did the same. We then followed the C & C, back to LZ Two Bits, while the Bird Dog began raining bombs and artillery onto the NVA.

Our unit always had to fly into areas that were totally inaccessible, to support an operation. The 1st Cav. would launch an operation way out in the middle of the mountains. They would start by air assaulting on to a mountain top with infantry, and then would fly in an artillery unit to provide canon fire where needed. The operation was so far from any base camps, that everything that would be needed, was put on to the mountain fire base by helicopter. The new camp would also include aviation assets. Huey lift ships, gunship, and scout birds all would move in. During these times we lived on the fire base, and usually slept in the helicopters or on the ground. We ate C rations heated on our little makeshift stoves, and flew around the clock.

If we were lucky, we would get hot meals that would be flown in by the supply helicopter, but most of the time we ate C-rations. The hot meals were lots of starches with gravy or sauce covering everything, like spaghetti or turkey loaf. They came in large insulated cans and everything was plopped onto a paper plate.

The C-rats came packed twelve meals to a case. Each meal was a neat little box of unknown food items, but were labeled as ham and lima beans, or pork chunks in gravy. The box had all the information printed on the side of the box, but if you were to open the twelve boxes and dump the contents of the cans, you could not identify what it was. Except for the lima beans. Each box came with a side dish of pound cake, or maybe some type of fruit, and a little packet of four cigarettes. You also got coffee and condiments and a small roll of toilet paper. *Save this last item. You will need it.*
I'm not saying these were old, but some of them were left over from WWII and Korea. I would open the condiment pack and find Lucky Strike cigarettes that were packed in the little green boxes from those war years.

The only fair way to dispense the C-rats, was to open the box upside down, and then select. That way no one could read what the meal was, and it was truly pot luck. A lot of trading went on with each meal, and everyone always tried to get the coveted can of fruit.

The air was so thin on the mountain top that the helicopters could barely fly. Heat, coupled with a heavy helicopter and no air for the blades to bite, made it difficult to get airborne. We would park right on the lip of the hill, so that if necessary you would get the bird barely moving, and then fall off the mountain. In that manner, you could gain airspeed and fly. Dangerous shit! I never practiced this in flight school.

You made sure to fire all of your rockets and machine gun ammo, and use up gas while out on a mission. That way the helicopter would be light enough on the return, to be able to come in and land.

Next to us were some gunships from the lift company. One of them tried the, "Fall off the hill and fly" technique, but got his skids caught in the concertina wire, which encircled the LZ. The ship just could not get off the ground. I hate to think what the last thoughts in those pilots minds were. They nosed over and tumbled down the mountain side, killing everyone on board.

This was truly a makeshift fire base. They had dug a trench, and placed a short platform on top of it, with cutouts for your butt cheeks. It did have a nice view though. I was sitting there reading the Stars and Stripes newspaper, and minding my own business. I heard someone sit down a hole away. A few minutes passed, and then this female voice said, "Please pass the toilet paper." I about shit. I did have a minor panic attack. She finished her business and left. I was not moving, until she was long gone. I pulled up my pants and found some people, to tell them about this strange event in the middle of the mountains. They just laughed. I was informed that this was the French journalist, Michele Ray, who traveled often with the infantry units. She ate, slept and followed the grunts around the jungle. Ms. Ray had been captured in January 1967 by the V.C, but was released a few days later, and was back to putting her fanny on the line to get a story.

We did a lot of flying in and around the mountains on the

Cambodian/Laos border with Vietnam. This area was absolutely beautiful, with lush jungle, rivers and waterfalls. We would do nap of the earth flying early in the mornings, up the sides of the mountains, following a river. I would come busting around the trees and find a river full of Montanyard women and children, all naked and taking a morning bath. It was like being back in the caveman times.

We landed on a grass strip way out on the border and parked, awaiting a mission. It was very hot so I stripped down to my tee shirt, and was sitting under the tail boom of the helicopter trying to find some shade. I lit up a cigarette and was taking things easy, when a Montanyard soldier came by. He stopped and then sat down next to me and began jabbering, but I couldn't understand a word he was saying. I had a letter from home and picture of Heleen, so I pulled out the picture and showed it to him. He smiled, and then pulled out a picture of a woman and two small children. I looked at it and smiled back. I then offered him one of my cigarettes and he accepted. We sat there not saying a word and smoked. A little while later he rose to leave, and then pulled out a pouch from his shirt. He extracted a hand rolled cigarette ,offered it to me, and I accepted. I lit it up as he wandered off, and the next thing I know I've got blurred vision and dizziness. *I think I also had the urge to eat a giant bag of potato chips.*

Whew! Was that thing strong? I told my crew chief and gunner that I couldn't smoke this, because it was so bad. The gunner, a surfer from California, jumped out of the helicopter and raced over saying, "Can I have it. PLEASE." I always harbored a suspicion that I may have been toking on a little home grown. This caused me to fail a polygraph a few years later, when applying to become a police officer. I had to explain why I kept answering no, when asked about smoking dope, and finally passed when the examiner re-phrased the question.

Flying near the border areas was like visiting the moon except for all the trees. Everywhere you looked there were these huge bomb craters from the B-52 strikes. They were going on continually, trying to stop the flow of men and supplies, coming down the Ho Chi Minh trail. A lot of the enemy movement was happening on the other side of the border, and of course we were forbidden from crossing over, and engaging the NVA. So whenever we finished a mission near the magic line and we had rockets left, we would point the nose west and pickle the rockets off. I don't think we hit anything, but it gave us satisfaction in violating the silly rules.

We were called into a top secret briefing during the missions by the border. A guy in civilian clothes, who was probably CIA, informed us that while flying near the Laos border, we may encounter NVA or Chinese MIG fighter planes, and if we did, we were not to engage them in air to air combat. They must have thought they were dealing with idiots, or maybe they knew the minds of teenage helicopter pilots. The briefer also said we may see enemy helicopters over the border, and we were not to chase them or engage them in anyway. "Let me get this straight. Wherever I fly, someone is shooting at my helicopter, but I can't reciprocate". Bullshit! Each and every one of us had visions of becoming the first and only "Helicopter Ace" in history.

*(1st Pilot) "What did you fly in Nam?"*

*(2nd Pilot) "I flew mail and chow out to the troops. What did you do?"*

*(1st) "Oh! I engaged a Mig 21 in air to air combat. Got the sucker on my second pass with my trusty M-16."*

Some war stories are just way better than others.

After a couple of weeks of this, we packed up and returned to LZ Two Bits. When we arrived back at base camp, the mess sergeant informed us that he had a special treat lined up, and that we needed to contribute a few dollars. He said it had been a while since anyone had fresh meat, so he had arranged to buy a baby water buffalo (Boo) from the *"Buffalo King of Vietnam."*

He bought this really cute little heifer, and staked him to a spot between my tent and the flight line. The mess crew was feeding him all kind of scraps and grass, with the intent of fattening him up. Every time I had to go to the aircraft or operations, or for that matter anywhere, I had to pass the baby Boo. I would stop and give him a hug, and pat him on the head and talk to him. Boy! Was that all the wrong things to do? After a couple of weeks the mess sergeant killed and butchered my new best friend, and then had a barbeque of water buffalo steaks. I couldn't eat a bite. Years later I was reacquainted with another pilot from the unit, Gordon Eatley. He had a picture of the baby Boo, and told me he couldn't eat a bite either.

We were on standby one night, and of course got called out on a fire mission. Some unit, somewhere was in contact with the enemy and needed assistance right away. The weather was absolute crap, and if we had been flying in the states, I'm sure we would not have been allowed to take off. But this was Nam, so off we flew.

We weren't in the air more than a few minutes when we entered into the clouds. I felt like I had just stuffed my head into a bag of cotton balls. Where we were flying, we were surrounded by mountains, so we had procedures in place if this should happen. The first thing to do, was the lead aircraft would turn right 90 degrees and start a climb, until he was above the clouds. The wingman would turn left 90 degrees, and do the same. You immediately needed separation from each other. I was flying and I could not see a thing. It was like being inside a small room, with the windows all painted white. The only point of reference was the instrument panel and lights. You had to believe the instruments because all of your senses told you that you are, turning, descending, climbing or upside down. You started believing this, and that is how pilots got vertigo and crashed.

I was trying to fly and keep us right side up, while climbing above the clouds. We had turned on our landing light, so that our wingman would at least maybe see this. Our sister ship called us, and told us that they were at 5,000 feet and had clear sky and the moon showing. We kept climbing, but were soon at 6,000 feet and still were in the clouds. Finally at 7,000 feet we broke out above the clouds, and now found out, our wingman had been right below us the entire time. They had been following our landing light. They were so screwed up and not believing their instruments, that they could have flown right into us and killed everyone.

Now we were above the clouds, and had no way to get back down. There was very little in the way of radar or beacons, for instrument landings, and none where we were. You also wanted to avoid finding a sucker hole. This was a hole in the clouds that would be maybe a few thousand feet deep, and you could see the ground. You would start down through one of these holes, only to have it close up, and there you would be back in the clouds, surrounded by mountains to run into. That's why they called them a sucker hole.

At our base camp we had jeeps on perimeter duty with xenon search lights mounted on the back, so they could light up the surrounding jungle. These lights were extremely bright, so we came up with the idea of using them to guide us in. We called the air field and had them get a hold of the jeeps. They positioned themselves at the end of the runway, with the lights shining up at a 45 degree angle. We homed in on the air field with our FM radio. The radio compass had a needle, which would point toward the source of the FM signal, and I could then fly toward that point. Back when the VC and NVA were new to our methods, they would be calling each other on FM radios. Gunships would home in on them, and deliver a nasty surprise. I got close and began flying in circles, and eventually picked up the lights, shining in the clouds. I then started a slow descent, following the light beam down to the back of the jeep. When I finally broke out of the clouds, I was right on top of the jeeps, and just had to go a few feet lower, to land on the air strip. I probably lost ten pounds that night, and had to get a change of underwear. I got out of the helicopter and could barely walk. My knees were shaking, and my stomach felt like there were a thousand butterflies trying to roost.

There were several stories around about helicopters that had gotten caught in the clouds, and were never heard from or seen again. We heard these stories in flight school, and as soon as we started flying in Nam, the incidents were reinforced. You would be out on a mission and hear a crew calling that they were lost in the clouds. No radar was available to help them, and they just didn't have an angel on their side. All radio transmissions from them would end. Sometimes ground units would stumble across a helicopter, crashed in the trees or on the side of a mountain. The crew and all the equipment would still be there. These places were so remote, that just luck would bring about their being found.

Some never were. Between 1962 and 1973, seventy six helicopter pilots were listed as Missing in Action. Most of these were due to the weather. They were all later declared Killed in Action.

# I LOVE AUTHORITY

Every mission I was on during this time seemed to turn to shit. One night we got called out to put rocket fire on some enemy troops, who were in contact with an infantry unit. There was a hell of a lot of gunfire going on when we called them up on the radio, and as we got closer, you could see all the tracer rounds going here and there. It was impossible to determine who was shooting at who, and where the friendly units were located. I can't remember the exact time of night, but it was dark. I mean so pitch black that you couldn't tell where the ground ended, and sky began. The unit in contact was down in the jungle, but was close to the mountains, so no low level attack could be done by the gunships.

The lieutenant I was flying with told me he knew where everyone was, and for me to set up for a rocket run. I told him I wasn't sure, and he told me to just do it. I backed off a few miles, and turned inbound toward the fire fight. I set up my rocket run, but kept telling this Lt. that I didn't know where I should shoot. We were almost on top of the fight, and this Lt. grabbed the controls. He then put the helicopter in a straight down dive, and started shooting off rockets. This can over torque the helicopter, and cause things to start falling off. Plus it was darker than the inside of Oprah's ass, and we had no idea where the mountains were. The crew chief and gunner were yelling on the intercom for the Lt. to pull up. Almost immediately, the ground unit started screaming, "Cease fire. Cease fire. You're hitting friendly troops!"

We broke off the run and I took the controls back from the Lt., and turned around to fly back to LZ Two Bits. Nobody said a word on the flight back, and we shortly started our descent into the re-fuel, re-arm area. When we landed I told the crew chief and gunner to unplug their helmets, and go stand in back of the helicopter. I then got out walked around the front of the bird, and opened the Lt's door. I slid back the amour plate, grabbed the Lt. and smacked him in the face. I told him if he ever did that again, I would kill him. I then walked back around to my side and got in. No one said a word, and we parked in our revetment, and shut down for the night.

A couple of days later, I was told by my platoon leader, that I was off flight status, and up on charges for assaulting the Lt. The commanding officer of my unit started an investigation, and brought in the crew chief and gunner. He also interviewed the Lt. who was in command of the ground unit, that we had been trying to help. After he heard the stories from everyone, he said that he was dismissing the charges, putting me back on flight status, and moving me to another helicopter. But now I had made two very determined enemies, and this would not be the end of things for quite some time. The lieutenant was of course a brother officer of my platoon commander, a captain. The captain did not have much use for warrant officers, and especially ones who behaved like me.

Extra duties were piled on me, and my life was made as miserable as the Capt. could make it, and stay within the army guidelines. The first thing he did was make me the property book officer for all of the helicopters. This in essence meant that each Huey and every single thing attached to it, belonged to me. I signed for them. If a rocket pod fell off in flight, and could not be found, I had to account for it. I totaled up the monetary amount of what I had on the books, and it came to about $11,000,000. That's a lot for a twenty-year old warrant officer to be responsible for. Especially since the regulations at that time made it clear that only a commissioned officer could be a property book officer.

I also got to be Officer of the Guard, and Officer of the Day. More time after flying, to spend not getting any rest. These were also commissioned officers duties, and were usually meant for those not flying all of the time.

During this period I was having a lot of difficulties with my molars, and this required me to fly back to An Khe, two or three times for dental surgery. I would fly back in the morning and have a tooth pulled, and then be back flying combat missions in the afternoon. This was mostly my wisdom teeth, and because of the loss of the teeth and the pain and discomfort, I was having problems eating. Especially, since we were eating the ever present C rats. My fellow pilots were kind enough to pull the easy to eat food out of the cartons, and pass it on to me. I collected a lot of the cans of fruit, and was virtually living on these. Of course, the asshole Capt. was taking notes, and this would come back to haunt me. Months later he would write me up for stealing the fruit from the C-ration boxes.

# SLEEP OF THE INNOCENT

Another fun mission we would do, was to join up late at night with a Huey slick, that was loaded with a search light and machine guns. The gunners were equipped with night vision glasses, and their machine guns were loaded with nothing but tracer rounds. There was a huge lake south east of Two Bits, out toward the South China Sea. It was believed, that the enemy was ferrying supplies across the lake, late at night by sampan. We would go out at 2:00 or 3:00 a.m with the slick, and fly blacked out across the lake. If they spotted a sampan, then it was assumed it was the enemy. All the local villages were told not to be out on the lake at night, but that was also the best time for them to catch fish. The Huey would open up on the sampan with the machine guns, to mark the location. The slick would turn on its search light, and circle the area keeping the boat lit up. I then rolled in hot, and sprayed the hell out of the area with rockets. I then broke right, and the door gunners would hose down the area with their M-60s. I would like to think that we stopped a lot of supplies, and killed a bunch of the enemy. I can't help believing, we probably blew the crap out of some poor fishermen, who were out there at night just trying to make a living.

Each evening, our unit would disperse the platoon's aircraft to different LZs. The platoon had twelve helicopters, but normally two would be in maintenance, for one reason or another. Of the remaining ten, three teams of two birds would leave. The reason for this was that if the other fire base got hit, then at least six gunships could get airborne, and bring death and destruction upon the enemy. This was not the best situation for the ships and crews, as we were just visitors to these bases, and no one had responsibility for our welfare. This meant that no unit provided us with such necessities as food, and a place to sleep.

Usually the crew chiefs would sleep in the copter and the pilots would find a vacant tent. I would end up sleeping on a couple of rocket boxes, with my air mattress and constant companion, the poncho liner. The poncho liner was a light camouflage blanket made from nylon, and was very warm. My problem was not my inability to sleep, as everyone will attest, I can sleep anywhere any time. It was my inability to be woken up. The fire base would get hit by mortars or rockets or even a perimeter probe by the V.C, and I would sleep right through it.

A lot of the tents we occupied were empty because they were situated either near, or right under the barrels of the large artillery pieces, that were firing all night long. No one else wanted them. Sometimes I would wake up in the morning, curled up in the corner of the tent wrapped in my poncho liner. The concussion of the large guns would literally blow me off the ammo boxes and air mattress, and send me across the floor. Everyone else would get up, and go find another place to sleep, but not me. I never would hear the guns go off. So this lead to the unofficial policy, of leaving me wherever I was, whenever something happened. Mortars would be coming in, and I would be sleeping. They figured it was better to lose me, than to risk losing anyone else, by trying to wake me up.

On one of our nightly dispersals to other fire bases, we got a call that a gunship was taking fire from an area next to a bridge, on Hwy 1, south of LZ Two Bits. This gunship put out a call on the emergency channel, and said he took a bunch of automatic weapons fire from a bunker, located next to the bridge. He asked for all available gunships in the area to meet up, and put fire on this bunker. So it wasn't long before our two gunships were in a big circle, which numbered about ten birds. We all took turns coming in hot, and shooting everything we had at this bunker. When everyone had pretty much ran out of bullets and rockets, we called it quits and continued on to where we would be spending the night. A couple of days later, we all got called in and we were told we were being courts martialed, for killing a bunch of Vietnamese soldiers at the bridge. Everyone explained what had happened, but it was decided we must be lying.

The story I heard later, was that the 1st Cav. decided to pay off the Viets for killing their soldiers and a bag man was sent to the regional, Vietnamese army post. He no sooner got there when he witnesses a bunker open fire, on a helicopter flying by. He asked what the hell was going on, and someone told him that some of the soldiers liked to do this as practice. The colonel packed up his bag of cash, and told the Viets to kiss his ass, and that was the last we ever heard of the shooting.

# FASTER THAN A SPEEDING BUFFALO

I always flew around 1,500 feet above the ground, so that I would be pretty much out of range of small arms fire. That is not to say that some bullets didn't go to 1,501 feet, and put a neat little hole in the airplane. It's amazing how loud a sound a bullet makes, when it hits the helicopter that you are flying. Loud sudden noises really get your attention. It's also not personal. At 1500 feet with a crew of four the bullets are always addressed, "To whom it may concern."

It's also amazing how quiet everything is when you are flying along, and the engine quits. One minute you are listening to the engine whining and the blades flapping, and maybe a little rock and roll on the Armed Forces Radio Network. All of a sudden the instruments read zero, and you can hear your heart beat. This is followed by everyone screaming like a Girl Scout troop, who has just had spiders dropped down their shorts. Then you start yelling for help on the emergency channel, for everyone within sound of your voice. And finally, prayers to God, that if he lets you land safe you will quit playing with yourself in the shower, looking at Playboy fold outs, and having impure thoughts.

We would on occasion take the helicopters down to low level, for simulated strafing runs on monkeys and water buffalos. These were conducted at about ten feet off the rice paddies, and sometimes even lower. It was not unusual for helicopters to come in from a flight with palm fronds hanging from some part of the bird. But what was really great sport, and endeared us to the local farmers, was when you would spot a rice field, with a water buffalo pulling a plow and a villager hanging on the back. If you could time it just right, you would pop up over a tree line and dive into the rice paddy behind the farmer. Before he knew what was happening, you would roar over the top of him and his four legged John Deere, scaring the be-Jesus out of both of them. Usually the farmer would go one way, and the water buffalo the other, but sometimes that little Asian cowboy would hang onto his plow and go for the ride of his life. We thought this was the funniest thing in the whole wide world, and then couldn't figure out why this guy would go home dig up his WW II rifle, and take a shot at a helicopter the next time he saw one.

We had some officers in the 1st Cav. with nothing better to do, than dream up new ideas for the use of helicopter gunships. One really neat plan was for the installation of two board chutes in the back of the bird, which were angled down and pointing out the side doors. They would install mortar rounds, stacked on top of each other, and pull the safeties. The plan was, we would fly over an area to be bombed, and then pull the release handle. This allowed the mortars to drop out of the back, and straight down to the ground. When you fired rockets at the jungle, which contained triple tree canopy, the rounds were ineffective and exploded on the top branches. The dreamers figured, that by dropping the mortars straight down, they would get through the trees, and impact the ground. In theory this should work, except for the mortars that got hung up in the chute, or fell without going off, or hit each other on the way down, causing shrapnel to fly around our airspace. It made the entire crew a nervous wreck each time we had to do this. I only did it a couple of times, and was glad when that mission was done.

Another fun outing, was when they loaded the chutes with CS gas grenades. These missions were not conducted at 1,500 feet where it was safe. They were flown at tree top level, where some yahoo in black pajamas, could knock you out of the sky with a rock. It was the same principal as the mortars, except it would require a couple of passes to unload everything, and you would have to fly back and forth through the gas cloud that you had made. This really tended to piss off the crew, who didn't have gas masks. One pilot would wear a mask, so that at least someone could see to fly the helicopter. If you ever get the chance to wear a U S Army gas mask, you find that they don't fit. They are very hot and uncomfortable and the rubber starts to rub the skin off your face. And they have these little glass eye holes, that don't look straight ahead, but off to the side. This causes some serious disorientation when trying to drive a plane.

The last experiment I was involved in did have success. A CH-47 Chinook would strap a couple of 500 gallon, rubber gas blivets under their bellies, and head out to a mountain where tunnels had been found. That pretty much meant anywhere in Vietnam. They would get some real good altitude, and the drop the blivets on the area. The gas tanks would burst, and gas and fumes would then seep into the tunnels. We would wait a few minutes, and then we would roll in and punch off white phosphorus rockets. When the explosions hit the gas and fumes, you could literally blow up a mountain and cause some serious cave- in action. I remember doing this a few times, and each time it would look like the mountain was made out of Jell-O. The ground would start to quiver and the trees would dance, and then the hill would sort of collapse upon itself, hopefully burying whoever was living in the caves.

# TOGETHER AGAIN

I got word from the American Red Cross, that I became a daddy on April 20th. I now have a shared parentage, of a little girl named Michelle. Mother and child were doing fine, and I couldn't wait until someone sent me pictures. Of course being twenty years old and flying combat, the stresses on me had quadrupled. I couldn't think straight, or eat much, and I had become a son of a bitch to try and get along with. I treated every order like it is a personal attempt to get me killed. Unless you go through something like this, you have no idea how traumatic life can get. I had a wife who had to go through a very difficult pregnancy without me, and now has given birth to our first child, who I have never seen or held. Plus, people are trying to kill me, which means I may never meet my child. Mean while, I am several thousand miles away from them, trying not to get shot, or crash into the side of a mountain.

I put in for R & R (rest and recuperation) in Hawaii, and was waiting for the approval. Unmarried personnel put in for A & A (alcohol and ass). I will be meeting Heleen in Honolulu, and she is going to be bringing lots and lots of pictures with her, of our new daughter, Michelle. A couple of weeks later, I got the orders sending me on a mini vacation to Hula Land. Heleen and I coordinated by letter and made hotel reservations. The big day arrived and I headed in from out in the field to An Khe to get cleaned up, and get my travel uniform and other clothes out of storage. They have all been packed away since I arrived in Vietnam. I had just enough time to get a haircut and a shower, and grabbed my gear and headed for the airfield. The next morning early, I will fly out of Nam for Hawaii, and I can't wait.

Early in the morning we were dressing in the semi dark, and packing what limited items of clothing we had. No one in their right mind brought civilian clothes with them to V.N. I mean where the hell would I wear them? Except, I found out that pilots not assigned to the 1st Cav. had civilian attire because they can wear them at night to the club, when they go to see a show, or maybe go downtown, for a dinner and drinks. There were two different wars going on in V.N. and I was not in the right one.

I grabbed my bag and started pulling out my tan travel uniform. What I had when I got to V.N., was a very nice tailored, tropical worsted shirt and pants. This was a classy looking uniform, and never failed to impress people. I looked like a poster boy for Army Aviation, when I had that uniform on. What I pulled from the bag, was a set of khakis, that must have belonged to the Jolly Green Giant. The pants were three inches too long and hung around my waist. I had been on an army diet for five months, and had a waist of about 28 inches. Those pants were more like a generous 34 inches. The short sleeved shirt was no better. The collar was going on 18 inches, and the short sleeves hung down to the middle of my forearms. The travel people were yelling at us to get our butts in gear or we "ain't" going to Hawaii, so I had no choice but to pull the khakis on, and run to the plane.

That was when I discovered that the zipper in the pants is blown out, and won't work. I had not entered my "no underwear" period, so I at least was not hanging out. We got on the civilian airliner, buckled up, and were soon airborne, going east into the rising sun. I was the only officer in the front of the airplane, and was surrounded by enlisted soldiers. Most of these guys really don't like officers, but they do love warrant officers, especially the ones who fly helicopters. The helicopter for most of them, is their life-line to the world. We bring them mail and movies, take out the wounded and sick, supply bullets and beans, and pick them out of the jungle for a ride to the airport so they can go on R & R.

A sergeant found out about my uniform problem, and before I knew it, several of them had me standing in the aisle while they surrounded me. Off came my pants, and they were handed to one of the stewardess, who took them up to the front of the plane. A couple of those ladies then took turns, doing a nice stitch job on the zipper. It wouldn't go up or down anymore, but now I was at least not open to the elements. I did not need the zipper anyway, because the pants were so loose, I could just pull them down if need be.

We finally arrived in Hawaii, and I was met at the airport by Heleen. All the wives were there on a bus to meet us and ride into Ft. DeRussy, where we had to process in. I kept getting slapped by Heleen, because she was wearing this nice little sun dress, and I couldn't seem to keep my hands to myself. We were in-processed and warned about missing the plane back to V.N., and then we were turned loose upon the population of Honolulu. Little did they know, that most of us did not venture far from the hotel rooms. We only surfaced to take in food, and maybe see a little of the tourist attractions. We did the cocktail show at Don Ho's, and I ended up being on stage, doing a hula with the show girls. Heleen and I rented a car for a day and toured the island. We drove out, around Diamond Head, and as much coast line as we could cover. We lay on the beach each day, and swam, and soaked up the sun. It all just went by, way too fast. This was the fastest seven days I ever spent. It seems like we landed, kissed our women hello and then kissed them good bye.

# BACK TO THE WAR

Things were no different when I returned. I was flying missions day and night, and three out of every four nights, flying off to spend the night in a strange LZ, with no bed. We basically ran two types of fire missions. If the G.I.s are going into an area to spend time looking for the enemy, we do a preparation (prep) of the LZ. The commander of the ground troops would find an area he wanted to put his men into. On the designated date and time, artillery would fire at the LZ and the area around it. As the troop helicopters would start into the landing zone, we would precede them and fire rockets into the area, where they were going to land. Then just in front of the troop ships would be the lift company gunships, that would also fire rockets and machine guns at all of the surrounding area. We would stay on standby until we either were called in for additional rocket runs, or were released to go back and refuel and rearm.

The other main mission I would get, would be to go out when someone needed our help. If a ground unit got hit or an LZ was in trouble, then I would fly out and try to put rockets on the bad guys. Sometimes I would be doing this all day and night. I would hit the enemy over and over until I expended all of my rockets, and then would head back in to rearm while another set of gunships would come out to take my place. We scrambled for one of these fire missions north of LZ English, and took another gunship section with us. There were four of us flying north, and we soon caught up to another pair of helicopters.

We were behind them about a mile and saw one of them just kind of come apart and go spinning into the ground, from about 2,000 feet up. It was the damnest thing. It looked like a large cloud of smoke appeared on the roof of the helicopter, and then it just came apart and went crashing into the rice paddy. The other ship started yelling about artillery fire and we immediately dove right, and down to the deck. Someone screwed up and flew us into an ongoing artillery barrage. Whenever you flew somewhere, you would call the Division Artillery and find out if they were shooting. You could plot where the guns were and where they were firing to, and then avoid that line. The big guns had a certain trajectory and you could fly under the arc (ill advised), or around them. Someone really screwed the pooch on this mission, and it cost us one helicopter and a crew of four.

When you were at a base camp, or on an LZ, the artillery would fire at pre-selected spots surrounding the base. This was called H & I fire (Harassment and Interdiction). There were presumed rally points and lanes of travel, for any enemy wanting to attack a fire base or LZ. These grid coordinates were plotted, and the artillery would fire rounds to those points, all through the night. This was to keep the enemy from forming up for an attack, but I think it was really to keep everyone awake.
*"Hey! If I have to be up all night with this big gun, I might as well fire it every once in awhile and keep you up too."*

The artillery would also fire illumination rounds. This was a large flare packed inside a shell casing. The entire thing would be fired into the sky where the flare would separate and float down beneath a small parachute. The shell casing was then free to go wherever gravity took it. One morning, we were summoned to the flight line to view the damage one of these casings made. A crew chief, who had been sleeping in the back of his helicopter, woke up because he smelled smoke. He sniffed around and found it was his bird that was smoking, so he called for fire extinguishers and help. A shell casing had dropped from the sky, and went through the roof of the helicopter, passing about a foot above the sleeping chief, and then down through the floor. It hit the battery on the way by, causing it to start smoking, before it buried itself in the ground. Jet fuel was leaking out, and potentially the entire helicopter could have gone up in a ball of fire.

A week later, we were notified that four gunships were going to go north, and join with other units to support the Marine Corp. The Marines had an air strip and a LZ up in I Corp and they needed the assistance of the 1st Cav., as they just couldn't manage by themselves. This was a fairly large LZ and was dominated on the east side by a mountain. When we arrived we were shown where to park and where we would be staying, and then we were informed that even though the Marines owned the LZ, and the top of the mountain, they did not own from ground level up. So if you were not careful and were just kind of standing around with your thumb up your ass, a sniper might decide to take a shot at you, and they were known to hit people now and then.

A real great feature of the Marine Corp. Field Doctrine, was that if you went on a hike into the jungle and encountered a little action, you could call for help. The only problem was that, they would have to form up another infantry unit, and they would march out to where you were, to rescue you. This may take a day or two, but what the hell, Marines don't mind. They didn't have the helicopter assets the Army had, so they just made due.

Marine helicopter assets were slim at best. When I arrived up north and started working their area, I noticed the perfect outlines of helicopters, burned into the rice paddies. It just seemed strange to be able to look down and see the outline of a Ch-46, a UH-1, or a Ch-34. We asked around about this phenomenon and learned that the Marines had sent their pilots-to-be; to the U.S Army Flight School, where they learned everything they needed, to become proficient aviators. That is, except for the class on autorotation. This is a very necessary part of flying, in that helicopters tend to quit flying when you least expect it, and the only safe way to land when the engine quits, is to autorotate. This maneuver is accomplished by gaining forward airspeed, which translates to lift. When you get near the ground you bleed off the airspeed, and then use the lift to cushion your landing. Marines didn't get this class. Seems the USMC was too eager to get them to Vietnam, so it cut short their training and figured they could learn as they go. A little OJT never hurt anyone, except maybe a flight crew. I was sitting in a shitter one day in Marine land, when I looked on the wall and there among all the other graffiti was the legend, "USMC. 192 years of proud tradition, unhampered by modern progress." Says it all right there, don't it?

While flying in support of the Marines, I got scrambled on a fire mission one day, to the northern part of their sector. We called the unit that needed help and then set up in our usual oval. One ship was always ready to roll in on the target, while the other ship was making his turn to come in and cover. That way we always had one helicopter facing the enemy. When you finished firing the rockets and started to break from the encounter, the door gunners would open fire to cover your rear, and then your sister ship would be inbound with his rockets. It really helped to keep the bad guys heads down.

I began my firing run and punched off about eight pairs of rockets, then began a right break. The gunner on the left was out on the skid, putting down suppressive M-60 fire, when all of a sudden he screamed that he had been shot. I swiveled around to take a look, and I saw him sitting on his seat holding his head. All I could see was blood around his face, and what looks like the insides of his noggin, splattered all over the padding around the transmission. I took a closer look and noticed feathers. "Feathers!" Who the hell has feathers in his cranium? Our gunner was leaning out in the slip stream, firing when he had a close encounter with a bird. The bird hit him right in the forehead area of his helmet, and splattered everywhere. He had his face shield down, and that blew apart, cutting him with the plastic shards. No wonder he thought he'd taken a round in the head.

It wasn't but a few days later, when two gunships from the lift unit scrambled on a firing mission. The 1st Cav. Flight Surgeon had decided to go along, and rack up a little flight time. Anyone on flight status had to get so many hours a month in the air, to earn their extra pay bonus. I think someone like the surgeon, had to have four hours a month to get their flight pay. The two helicopters headed out to where the action was, and as soon as they arrived they started taking incoming rounds. As they made a gun run and began their break, the lead bird with the surgeon on board took hits through the bottom. The pilot in the right front seat got splattered all over his neck with a thick sticky mess, and quickly assumed the flight surgeon had taken a hit in his head. The story about our crew chief was still fresh in everyone's mind. He thought he had brain matter all over, and immediately began throwing up on his boots. Then came the laughter. The crew chief had just been to mail call, and had received a package from home. The scramble for the mission occurred before he could take his box to his tent, so he stuffed it under the seat in the helicopter. When they took the incoming enemy fire, a round hit the new jar of creamy peanut butter, and sent the contents flying everywhere. The only battle casualty that day was Skippy.

When we finished our little adventure with the Marines, we headed back down the coast toward Two Bits. We spotted some boats running south, about a quarter mile out to sea and went out to take a look. These were Navy gun boats which looked to be about 40 feet long. The crew started waving to us, so we decided to pay them a little visit. I flew toward the stern of one of the boats, and as I got close, I dropped my speed down to match the boats. I was now flying about ten feet off the water, and had the nose of the helicopter right over the back of the boat. The navy crew then began filming us, and my co-pilot took my movie camera and did the same to them. I sure would like to find the navy guys and trade film with them.

The only fun time we had was about once every month we would take two helicopters down to the Song Lai Giang river which, was just south of LZ Two Bits. We would load the crew chief and door gunners, maybe a couple of guys from maintenance or the mess hall, and they would all bring their guns to provide security. This was really a thinly disguised way to get them off the LZ, and give them a little fun.

We would land in the river on a sand bar, and then strip naked. While we took turns swimming, and washing the helicopter, the others would stand guard. Then we would switch. Normally the crew and guards didn't want to trade, because as soon as we landed the local villagers and hookers would show up. A lot of the little kids would be climbing all over the helicopter and helping to wash it, and you had to watch them like hawks, or they would steal everything not nailed down. Then the villagers would bring out the cold beer, and the guards would start bargaining for 15 minutes in the bushes with one of the girls. It was a great time to blow off a little steam and maybe get a bath. I guess the local V.C figured we needed a little time off, as I never heard of anyone at the river being bothered, or shot at.

In June I got called in and was told to report to the Division Artillery Commander, Colonel George Putnam. Col. Putnam told me that my platoon commander, the captain, had written me up for cowardice (I went to the dentist to avoid flying). Insubordination (I smacked that stupid lieutenant), and theft (I stole and was hoarding fruit from the C-rations). Col. Putnam told me that he had a hard time believing all of this, and he wanted to hear my side of the story.

I sat with him for an hour or so, and related all of the incidents, and told him that if he was to ask the other pilots, they would back me up. He said he needed a couple of minutes to think, and then told me he was transferring me to another unit. He said he believed me and would make sure everything turned out alright for my career. I was told that I was being transferred to E Battery, 82nd Artillery. I had no idea what the hell this outfit was, but I packed my stuff and crossed the air strip to join them. I had finally managed to piss off the captain enough, that he figured a way to get rid of me.

It turned out that I will be going from a fully loaded Cadillac, with all the bells and whistles, to a jalopy that does not even have doors. I never flew anywhere without another pilot, and at least one door gunner with an M-60 machine gun, and I usually had another ship along to keep me company. Now I will be by myself most of the time, with nothing but an M-16 tied to the door.

*Maybe I could go back and kiss and make up with the captain.*

# OH-13 SIOUX SCOUT

# SPADS

The first thing I notice is, that I now will be flying the lovely OH-13 which made its Army debut in 1946, and first saw combat in the Korean War. Remember watching MASH on T.V. or the "Batcopter" from the Batman series. Same helicopter only mine was newer. The army was also using them for instrument training at Ft. Rucker, AL. These 13s were slightly newer, and had turbo charged engines, but were just a two man helicopter, with a great big bubble in front of the pilot. I checked in and found a few guys that I had gone to flight school with. Jim Klod, Gordon Eatley, Bill Hyler had all been in my flight class and now we were flying together again.

The 82nd had a great bunch of pilots. The unit was mostly warrant officers, but we did have a few officers. The officers flew the fixed wing Bird Dog planes (A two seat, Piper Cub. One man in front, one stuffed in the back), that were assigned. The warrants got the H-13s. The mission of the 82nd was to provide reconnaissance, and direct fire support for the 1st Cav. artillery units. Most of the time I would take off with an artillery officer as my door gunner/artillery spotter. I would go out to where the infantry was humping through the jungle, and I would fly low and slow above them, to either draw fire, or try and spot the enemy. My artillery lieutenant would then call in the big guns to blow the shit out of the area. I use to fly at 1,500 feet and shoot rockets at the jungle. Now I was at five feet, and my weapon system is an M-16 stuck in the door frame. The doors were taken off the H-13 and there were two hinges attached to the opening. I hooked the front sight of the -16 on the lower hinge, and put the butt of the gun next to my left hip. To zero the weapon, I would find a safe area and land, then fire a magazine or two. When I determined where the bullets were going, I would draw a circle on the bubble. All I had to do was line up the circle on the target and shoot, then punch the magazine release when empty, and slam in another full one. Most of the artillery Lt's would carry an M-60 machine gun, and act as the door gunner, but a lot of the time I would be on my own.

I normally went out on a mission with the -16, and a box of grenades on the seat next to me. I had fragmentation grenades, plus smoke and white phosphorus. If I needed to, I would hook the grenade ring on the upper door hinge, pull the pin loose, and drop the grenade on the target below me. This was seat of the pants, WW I flying, and being up close and personal with the enemy.

When I first came into the Cav. I talked about the 1/9 Cav. and the scout unit. They flew the same H-13 I did, but theirs was armed with machine guns on the skids, and a door gunner with an M-60. They also had a Huey gunship flying behind them at all times, in case they drew fire. They were more aggressive in looking for the enemy than we were in the 82nd as that was their sole job. But they also had more fire power at their disposal. I guess my being young and dumb did have its advantages. At one time our H-13s were equipped with skid mounted M 60's, but the pilots kept getting themselves in trouble with them, so they took them away. We were still getting in trouble, but now we were not nearly as well armed.

Shortly after I became part of the 82nd another pilot from my old unit showed up to be a scout pilot. He told me that he was tired of flying around way up in the air and firing rockets, and he was bored. He got trained up and started flying missions with a crew chief gunner. On his second mission out, he was low level over the trees, when he took a round that almost killed him. He was heard to remark, "Be careful what you wish for." The crew chiefs were all given basic flight instructions by the pilots, in case they needed to fly the ship if we were wounded. It was almost needed that day.

The 82nd was based out of LZ Two Bits, but we always had a couple of ships stationed elsewhere. Wherever the Cav. was fighting they would construct a new LZ, and take artillery units with them. So we tagged along to provide the needed support for the ground units. My typical day might start with an artillery lieutenant showing up, to inform me that a unit of American soldiers at such and such a location were heading for another spot, but were taking some enemy fire. I would fly out to where they were and contact them on the radio, and then I would start flying in front of them, and acting as a guide dog. If we spotted enemy troops, we would notify the ground unit; fire at the enemy, and drop smoke grenades to mark the location. Then I would back off, and my Lt. would call in artillery strikes on the bad guys' positions. Then we would start all over again. If I ran low on ammo and gas, another bird might come out and relieve me, or if we were short handed the ground unit would form a perimeter until I could return. I would then run back to the nearest base to rearm and refuel. This was usually done while the helicopter was still running. I didn't have time to shut it off, and then restart it. This did make for some interesting times.

# HEMORRHOID HARRY

I got a call that one of the pilots had been injured, and they didn't know what was wrong, except they found him unconscious next to his helicopter. It turned out, that like the rest of us he came into refuel and left the bird running. The H-13 had two gas tanks that were located on top of the engine, just behind the bubble where the pilot sits. There was one on each side, and required the pilot to fill one side, then drag the hose around to the other side and repeat the fueling. All of this was done with the pilot standing on the skid, with his head up near the rotor blades. Well dumb Harry, the injured pilot, got distracted and stood a little too high. He stuck his nozzle into the rotor blades and got knocked on his ass. If he hadn't been wearing his flight helmet it, would have killed him.

Harry was the most obnoxious person I had ever met, but he was also one of the best H-13 pilots in the army. Harry would walk up to you and start talking, and within two minutes you wanted to punch his lights out. I remember one time when Harry flew to some fire base, and lo and behold there was Charlton Heston, the movie star, doing a meet and greet with the troops. Harry got to the front of the line and started in on Heston, telling him what he thought about movie stars and civilians in general. Within moments they had to restrain Heston from punching Harry.

Harry liked to play practical jokes on the other pilots, but none of the jokes were funny. They were all mean spirited and only served to piss everyone off. One of the pilots had it with Harry, and decided to teach him a lesson. At that time, all of us pilots carried .38 revolvers, so Dooley (a fellow warrant) took one of his bullets and pulled the lead out of the casing. He then stuffed a cigarette filter in the bullet, and put it back into his gun. It didn't take long before Harry started in on someone about something, and it started to escalate.

Dooley then walked up to Harry and told him he was tired of all of his shit, and if he didn't stop it, he would kill him. Harry turned his attention on Dooley and said some sarcastic comment. Dooley whipped out his gun and told Harry he was a dead man. With that, he pulled the trigger. The cigarette filter flew out and hit Harry in the chest. Harry thought he was dead, and fell down screaming. We all thought it was the funniest thing we had ever seen, and we were rolling around with tears in our eyes. This event put Harry in his place for about two weeks, and then he was right back to being an asshole.

We all flew with our M-16 tied to the door and the box of grenades on the seat next to us. I would sometimes take a fragmentation grenade and hook the ring on the door post hinge, and then pull to arm the grenade. I could then drop it straight down onto a target. Well Harry tried this one day, and dropped the grenade on the floor at his feet. The grenade rolled forward, and down into the bubble. Harry said he watched it roll back and forth a couple of times, while thinking he was going to be responsible for shooting himself down. There is an inspection plate in the bottom of the bubble, and it was used to clean the dirt out of the bubble. Thankfully the crew chiefs took these out and left them out. That way, when it rained the helicopter would not fill up with water. Luckily the grenade dropped through the inspection plate, and blew up just under the helicopter, where it did some minor damage, but not enough to disable the ship.

Like all good Vietnam helicopter pilots, who were flying every day and night, Harry suffered from hemorrhoids. Harry would complain continually about his affliction, and was always crying that he flew too much or too often, and that he needed medical attention. This went on for several weeks, when finally the commander told Harry to fly down to the hospital at Qui Nhon, and get them taken care of.

When Harry returned a couple of days later he told us his story. Obnoxious Harry, walked into the emergency room at the army hospital, and of course started pestering doctors to do something about his hemorrhoids. These doctors, were of course busy tending to wounded soldiers, and kept brushing Harry off. If nothing else Harry was persistent and kept after the doctors. Finally one of them told him to walk down the hall to another hall, then take a left and a right, and there he would find the doctor's office. The doc told Harry that as soon as he finished up, he would be down to take a look at Harry's ass and see what could be done. Harry found the office and made himself comfortable. After an hour or so the doc showed up and told Harry to drop his pants, and get up on all fours on the examination table, so the doc could take a look. Harry said the next thing he knew, the doc had a hold of his hemorrhoids, and snipped them off. No warning and no anesthesia. Harry said he screamed so loud, and so long, that they sent people to the doctor's office to see what the hell was going on. The doc slapped a bandage on Harry's bleeding ass, and put him to bed for 24 hours. Then they packed him up, and told him never to show his face at the hospital again.

But Harry could fly the rotors off that H-13. One day Harry was assisting a ground unit who was in a pretty big fire fight with the VC. The Americans had taken casualties and had wounded that needed to be medevaced out, or they might die. Without any thought to his own safety, Harry flew into the middle of the battle with his underpowered helicopter, built to hold two people. He picked up three wounded soldiers, and somehow stuffed them all in the cockpit, and flew them to the hospital. The H-13 in Vietnam was not the most powerful helicopter. Sometimes with two people in it you had to bounce it down the runway just to get it airborne. You would bounce-bounce-bounce until you bounced high enough in the air, then you would nose over and try to gain air speed. With airspeed you could then gain lift, and fly. Harry had four in his bird and was down in the jungle in the hot afternoon. Not the best conditions to try and fly, and it was truly an amazing feat. Harry got the Distinguished Flying Cross for his actions that day.

# SHITTIN SLIVERS

This of course was not the only character in the unit. With the missions we did, it was only natural to have a whole bunch of pilots, who may have come up as slightly deranged on any psychological profile. There was Jim Dooley who liked to eat glass and do other assorted tricks to garner attention. He could take a light bulb or a highball glass and reduce it to the stem. Jim and I would go into a bar, and he would push his way in amongst the majors and Lt. colonels. They would give him a look, but do nothing else because of his size and intimidating demeanor. Most of the time we were wearing either a ratty flight suit, or jungle fatigues which had seen much better days. Water was a scarcity with us, and was used for drinking. Clothes and humans didn't get to see much of it for washing. Being in the 1$^{st}$ Cav. also meant that you went nowhere without a gun or guns, and probably a bandolier of M-16 magazines. Anyway, Jim's next move would be to pick up someone's drink off the bar, slurp it down and then slam the glass back down to make sure he had the owner's attention. As soon as he got the look from some officer or was questioned as to who the hell he thought he was, he would pick up the empty glass and take a bite out of it. Then he would stand there calmly and bite and chew until the glass was gone. It was about then that people would start buying Jim and I drinks.

The Chu Lai AFB Officers Club, on the hill above the South China Sea was beautiful. We didn't get there often, but when we did we always made it a memorable event. The club was occupied, mainly by air force personnel and army officers, who didn't see much action, if any. So they were always looking their best and we were always looking our worst. Plus, as mentioned the club was always telling us not to bring our guns into their club and our response was always, "If you want them, then you can come over here, and take them off of us." Being hard core crazed killers, we didn't take shit from anyone. Especially those whose idea of war, was having to get up from their air conditioned bedroom, and maybe go outside to their bunker, should the V.C be so uncivil as to lob a rocket at the air base.

I remember one night we were in the club, and of course being 20 years old, and a little inexperienced at drinking hard liquor, we became just a bit unruly. I don't recall just what started the "challenge", but soon we were playing horsy and trying to knock the other teams over. I was mounted on Dooley and there were maybe four other teams, and we were really interrupting the hell out of the other peoples war stories. Some club manager came running over, and was yelling at us and telling us he was going to have us thrown out, and maybe even arrested.

The Chu Lai Club was made out of bamboo and other assorted wood, and had a woven grass roof. Out came the Zippos from the assembled fighters, and the club manager was told we would burn his club down, if he didn't leave us alone. Being a smart college graduate, who must have had some courses in decision making and conflict resolution, the manager made the decision to buy us all drinks, if we would behave.

That brought a speedy halt to the night's festivities. I mean who wouldn't want free drinks?

# REAL OFFICERS DON'T CRY

Another of the unwashed, undisciplined, warrant officers was Randy Bell, who could bench press a six pack. Randy was not our poster boy for physical fitness, and was always being picked on by the lieutenants and captains, that were in our unit. They had their own tent, but always chose to walk through the warrant officer's tent, on their way too or from the shitter or shower. This gave them the opportunity to harass the warrants, and pick on Randy in particular. We had this one Capt. who never let a chance go by to tell us that he was smarter, taller, prettier, more athletic, a better flyer and all around great guy, and of course, could do anything Randy could do, and do it better.

One afternoon we were done flying, and sitting around the tent having a beer and bullshitting, when in walked the Capt. on his way to take a shower. He had nothing on but flip flops and a towel, but stopped to get in Randy's face. Randy was sitting in his Vietnam lounge chair, drinking a beer, and listened while the Capt. went on and on about how great he was compared to Randy.

The Capt. left and went down the hill to take a shower. About twenty minutes later the Capt. reappeared all clean and shiny, but had to come through our tent, to take another shot at Randy. The Capt. started in, but Randy stopped him and said, "I'll bet you a case of beer that I can do twice as many pushups as you can." With that the Capt. dropped down to the dirt floor and started doing pushups. Pretty soon he was sweating and kicking up dust, which was now coating him in a nice red patina. I think I heard him say he did twenty five or so pushups, and now it was Randy's turn to do twice that. Randy looked at the now dirty Captain and replied, "I am totally out of shape, and don't think I can do five pushups, but I will be over later with your case of beer." The rest of us were laughing so hard I thought we'd puke, and all of us were talking trash to the dumb Capt. who was so embarrassed, he didn't even go down to take another shower. Of course that kept him out of our tent and our lives for a couple of weeks, before he started in again.

We played a lot of poker to pass the time at night. We had a light bulb that hung down at one end of our tent, so that was where the poker table was set up. And of course you couldn't play poker unless you were drinking a lot of beer, because that makes you a smarter poker player. Whenever it rained we had a mongoose who didn't like to get wet, so he would come into our tent. He would scamper about, and then get up on the ropes that held the mosquito nets over the bunks, and run around. He wasn't tame or anyone's pet, but he just preferred hanging out with the warrant officers when it was dark and stormy outside. One night we were playing cards and drinking, and it started pouring down rain. Pretty soon the mongoose showed up and began his exploration of the tent. Ron Pincock had drunk a little too much, so we carried him down and laid him on his bunk, so we could listen to him snore and fart. Someone said, "Hey look at the mongoose. I think he's going to bite Ron." The mongoose was walking around and around the head of Ron's bunk. These were regular army cots that had wooden cross members, and a canvas stretched across them. Most of the guys were sleeping with their heads in toward the center aisle and their feet pointed out, and this was how Ron was laid out. Jim said he was going down to see why the mongoose was going to eat Ron, and maybe chase him off. Jim was just a shade less drunk than Ron, and most of us were not far behind, so we all thought this was a splendid idea. Jim got down to Ron's cot and there on the cross member by Ron's head, was a bamboo viper. This was what the mongoose had his eye on. Jim thought the critter needed some help, so he went to his bunk and got his .38 and a box of bullets. He returned to Ron's area, and sat down on the bunk across the aisle from Ron. He then took careful aim, and fired six times at the snake. With the first round the mongoose exited from the tent at a high rate of speed, and was never seen again. Jim reloaded and fired another six, then reloaded again. Jim fired eighteen rounds before scaring the snake to death, and to his credit, did not hit Ron or even wake him up.

Poker night again and some brews to help us count the cards. We were all set to enjoy each other's company, and maybe tell tales of the days daring flights. The sides of our tent were rolled up so that we could get a little air through there, if a breeze was blowing. The perimeter of the tent was always sand bagged up to about three feet to provide protection from incoming small arms fire or rockets. With the sides rolled up, there was a gap of about two feet from the top of the sand bags to the bottom of the rolled tent. All of a sudden, the entire top of the sand bags erupted with pops and bangs, and a whole bunch of flashing. We all thought that VC had got into the camp, and were firing machine guns at us. Everyone hit the dirt, and someone smashed the light bulb. The next thing I knew, we were overcome by CS gas inside the tent. We were all choking and couldn't see, so we all tried to get out of the tent, from the nearest door, at the same time. Our tent was surrounded by rolls of concertina wire, and there was a small gap so that you could enter and exit through the wire. We were all pushing, shoving, choking, crying, and yelling that we were going to die, and of course piled on top of each other into the wire. Now we were caught in the wire, and getting all cut up trying to get out, and still couldn't see a damn thing.

Eventually help arrived and got us untangled and that's when we found out that another group of warrant officer aviators, thought it would be fun to sneak over and pop gas grenades in our tent. I heard that the ass chewing they got was beyond belief, and that most of them had to stand up to fly for a while.

There was a major assigned to the unit next to us who was a royal dick head. He had no impact on our lives, but he made everyone else around, jump to his insane orders or directives. Wear your helmet to see a movie. Wear a flak jacket while having breakfast. Always have your weapon with you, but do not load it. The list went on and on, and we were always hearing the enlisted men bitching about the major. The grunts were the special target of the major, and we figured that he had a real bad attitude toward them for some reason. Maybe he had been passed over for promotion, or he wanted a combat command and couldn't have one. Who knows?

We were situated on a small hill, and below were the community shitter and shower point. The facilities were not located right on the concertina wire perimeter. They were close enough that you could sit and look out over the wire at the jungle, which was maybe a couple of hundred yards away. One night the major went down for his usual bowel movement, with a Stars and Stripes Newspaper in hand. It was not more than about five minutes and we heard screaming, yelling, and crying, coming from down by the wire. The major, who had been sitting facing out toward the surrounding jungle, had been shot in the ass with a cross bow dart. Though in no danger of dying, he was in a lot of pain, and was letting everyone know about it. It was called in as an enemy attack, with only one friendly W.I.A., and not a single round of American fire in response. The major was awarded a Purple Heart for wounds received during an enemy attack, and a Bronze Star for defending the perimeter against hostile invaders. He was then transferred out, and never heard from again.

We also had an infamous lieutenant, who had been going to the village of Bon Son on a regular basis, and visiting a bar and whore house. Now it would appear that he had contracted some strange sores on his wee wee (warrant officer pilots have dicks. Lieutenants have wee wee's). It had become great sport to not only taunt him and point fingers, but it was like a side show, watching him pee. He stepped up to the piss tube and then pulled a pair of white cotton gloves from his pocket. After putting them on he unbuttoned the fly on his jungle fatigues, and then started jumping up and down until his "wee wee" flopped out. The Lt. then urinated holding his manhood with two fingers, and when finished pulled out a tube of ointment. He then smeared this salve onto his wee wee, and then started the hopping routine, until he had it back inside his pants. He then rebuttoned, wiped the pain induced sweat from his brow, took the gloves off and went on with his business. No one will shake hands with this man.

*"Hey I'm going on a dangerous mission. Put it there."*

*"Uh! No thanks."*


There must have been a dozen of us pilots during this period and we were all flying every single day. The hours got long and the missions were hairy, but the perverse sense of humor never was far. I don't care what unit you were flying for, what your mission was, or even when you may have arrived "In Country." If anyone found you were headed out for a mission with an element of danger, the requests started to pile on.

"Can I have your stereo if you don't come back?"

"How about your bunk?"

"Can I have your wife, girlfriend, car, air conditioner, fan, chair"?

It didn't matter. Everyone would lay claim to everything you had of value. It was macabre humor at its best.


At Two Bits we had a mess tent, and if you timed things right, you could get a hot breakfast or dinner. Hot, real food was better than hot C-rations, which are better than cold C-rations, which are better than no food at all. Lunch was usually leftover's made into sandwiches. And of course everything was either canned or dehydrated. Powdered eggs, powdered milk, mystery meats. All the comforts of home.

We discovered care packages during this time. I can't remember who got the first one, but a family member had sent a Hickory Farms package, that contained cheese and a beef stick, plus assorted crackers and mustards. We all shared in this mini buffet, and decided we needed more. So we all took to writing everyone we could think of. Mom and Dad, wives, girlfriends, aunts, uncles. No one was beyond our reach, and just to make sure the letter got immediate attention, we added little hints about our desperate situation. I would take my letter and smear a little mud on it, and maybe pick a scab or stick my finger with a pin. A little blood dripped on the bottom, with a plea for goodies, was not beyond the bounds of decency, and highlighted the horror of war. It wasn't long before we started getting these nice little presents in the mail. We would hoard them for a week or so, until we had a stockpile, and then the feast would begin. Out came the booze, and we would sit around the poker table and stuff ourselves. I never knew there was any type of cheese other than Velveeta, until these packages started arriving. Now I'm eating Gouda, Swiss, Limburger, and who knows what else, plus the beef stick on crackers with mustard. It all got washed down with a few beers.

Of course every rainbow has a rock in it. I think everyone of us ended up with diarrhea. It took a couple of days to get the old digestive tract back to where it was supposed to be. Then we waited for the next shipment of goodies, and did it all over again.

# MOVIN NORTH

I moved north of Chu Lai to a hill called LZ Baldy. Baldy was primarily an artillery base, and was located near Hwy 1. Hwy 1 ran north and south from the bottom of Viet Nam, up into North Vietnam. There was a lot of action going on in this area and it was crawling with North Vietnamese soldiers. At Baldy we had two helicopters, two pilots and two crew chiefs. We were living in a couple of small tents and tried to make it a home. Our little camp was located close to the concertina wire that separated us from a small village. The first thing we did was put up sand bag walls for the two helicopters, and then we built a fighting bunker between the birds and the wire. Lastly we sandbagged the tents and started building ourselves a real shower.

Most of the time when I was in the field, I didn't have a shower, or for that matter much water in which to take one. I would wait for the rain to come and would run outside naked, with a bar of soap. Sometimes I would finish and other times the rain would quit, so I would end up with soap drying all over me. I would then stand out there buck naked, scanning the sky for another rain shower. If I was lucky, it would rain again, and I would start foaming and turn into a big soap bubble. Hurry and rinse and I was done.

Now we were in large LZ and water shouldn't be a problem. We scrounged up some lumber and decided to build a shower. We erected a stand about seven feet tall. On top we placed a 55 gallon barrel and filled it with water, then connected a hose and shower head, out of the bottom. The army provided us with everything we needed to have a hot shower. Potato chips were sent to the mess halls in five gallon aluminum cans. I got a can and filled it half way with dirt to provide ballast, and then I would siphon off a gallon of gas from the helicopters. Gas was poured on top of the dirt and lit on fire. This would burn long enough to heat the water, and then I could take a shower. Ingenious!

I used a similar method to heat food whenever the army provided me with a day of camping in the jungle. I always carried a can with me about the size of a soup can. I cut some vents in the sides and would fill it with dirt. Then get a little gas from the H-13, light it off and place a can of ala C ration on top. Voila! Hot meals.

We had the shower all rigged up and were enjoying it immensely, when fate shit in my mess kit. It was just after dark a couple of weeks later, when from the village area, you could hear the distinctive sound of mortars being dropped down the tubes. There is no other sound like it, and you come to recognize it quickly. Next you had to determine if it's our mortars going out, or the enemy's mortars coming in. There was not much doubt about this, as our mortars were on the hill to our rear, and these rounds were coming from the other side of the wire. I grabbed my rifle, bandolier of magazines, and flak jacket, and decided to run for our bunker. We had constructed a sandbagged pathway which zig zagged out the doorway of the tent. This was done to prevent incoming bullets or shrapnel from entering the tent. The two helicopters set a little ways from our tent facing the village, and in front of them was the bunker.

The mortars were coming in and you could hear them whistling. I ran like my ass was on fire toward the bunker, when the first mortar round hit right in front of me. I learned later, when I woke up, that it was probably five to ten feet from me when it landed. The round exploded and knocked me unconscious, and sprayed the shrapnel in a V, hitting both helicopters and doing a lot of damage. I didn't get a scratch on me, and have no idea how that missed killing me. One of the next rounds hit our new shower and blew it down, and both tents were riddled with holes. I tend to think that the V.C had been watching our efforts from the village, and were jealous about the comforts we had established. They targeted us with the sole purpose of making us have to take rain showers again. Maybe they just liked seeing us naked, and dancing in the rain.

My unit pulled the two -13s out and sent them for repairs, and for a couple of days I had nothing to do. Then I got a call that said they were sending a Bird Dog up from Two Bits to pick me up and fly me down. They had another helicopter waiting for me and I needed to come down, and fly it back to Baldy. A lieutenant arrived at the air field and helped me get into a parachute. I had never had one on before and it felt strange. You just don't get to jump out of helicopters. He finally had me all trussed up, and then he stuffed me into the back seat of the Bird Dog. I can only see out the sides and he's telling me what I need to do if I have to bail out. We took off and this smart ass climbs to about twenty five feet, and flies the whole trip in the tree tops. If we had crashed they could have used the parachute to bury me in.

 A few days after the mortar attack, a major was walking around the base when he spotted our Vietnamese barber, sitting on a large rock on top of the hill. The major walked over and peered across the barber's shoulder, and watched as he was sketching in all of the positions on the LZ. The barber was so intent, that he didn't notice the major until it was too late. I never got another hair cut from that guy. He just disappeared.

One of my extra duties was to train the new artillery lieutenants on how to stay orientated to the ground while flying low level, and how to adjust the big guns while doing circles above the tree tops. I would get the Lt. strapped into the helicopter, give him a map and point out where we were currently at. I would then take off and start flying around the area, while down in the trees and rice paddies. After about fifteen minutes of this I would ask the Lt. to show me where we were on the map. I never had one figure out where we were on this first flight. They would point at some spot on the map that may or may not still be in Vietnam. I would then pop up to a couple of hundred feet, and there would be LZ Baldy right where we had left it.

During the initial briefing I also made it clear to them that they might get airsick during this ride. They would all shake their head and tell me that being airsick, was not in their vocabulary. The crew chief would also tell them that if they did get sick they had to clean up the helicopter. A few did puke on their boots, but all of them cleaned up their mess. Once they got use to flying low level and doing the twists and turns they were fine. I never had one throw up after the initial flight, though I may have made a few have to change their pants.

They eventually got the hang of following the map while zooming through the jungle, and most of them were a really nice bunch of guys to work with. Although I do not think they were all that bright. Most were older than I was and had been to college, or at least had seen some of the world. Now here they were, strapping themselves into this tiny, bullet magnet, and allowing themselves to be flown through the trees, by some immature warrant officer.

# THE LITTLE ENGINE THAT COULD

I was sitting in my tent one morning, when an artillery major came running in and said that a convoy had gotten ambushed on Highway 1, and he needed to get there right away. I strapped on all my guns; knives; bullets; grenades; and chicken plate, then waddled out to my -13 and cranked it up. We lifted off and I started north, and after about ten kilometers, spotted some jeeps and trucks stranded on the road. It looked like at least one truck had gotten hit by a hidden bomb, much like the current IED's (improvised explosive device) that are so popular in Iraq and Afghanistan. There were a couple of bodies laid out on the road and a bunch of marines crawling around near the convoy. I checked the wind, and came down and landed on the road so the major could talk to them, and find out what was needed. We didn't have each other's radio frequencies so we were unable to communicate air to ground. I landed and a marine sergeant came crawling over to my side. He started yelling that we were being shot at from the village to our rear, and we might want to skedaddle. He also said that is where the wires from the IED were headed.

I lifted off quickly and turned toward the village, which was maybe 100 to 200 yards from the ambush. I stayed at about three feet off the ground and made sure that my M-16 was locked and loaded, and the safety was off. The major had an M-16 also, but was busy with his maps and talking to the artillery unit back at LZ Baldy. I got into the village and was hovering around real slow, and peaking into huts and behind walls and trees. I didn't see so much as a chicken or a dog. There was absolutely no one home, and this should have alerted me more than it did. I kept moving around, and spinning in circles so that I could cover myself, but didn't see a single living thing. I told the major that everyone must have gone di di and that I was heading back to the highway.

I was still at about three feet when right below me was a hole, with an NVA soldier laying on his back and aiming an AK-47 straight up. I didn't have time to go up, down, stop or accelerate. He let loose with the entire thirty round banana clip, right into the bottom of the helicopter. The entire inside of the -13 was riddled. The radios were blown out as were all the instruments. The bubble looked like Swiss cheese, and the floor resembled a pasta strainer. When the instrument panel got shot up it cut the fuel and oil lines coming into the cockpit and fluids were spraying all over me. I also knew that the rotor blades and engine were damaged, but for now I was still flying.

My right calf took a hit and knocked my foot off the rudder pedals. I was now flying sideways because I now had full, left pedal shoved in. The blow was so intense that I was afraid to look down, because I knew my foot was blown off. My entire right side was on fire from my ankle to my shoulder from all the shrapnel I had been hit with. The major started screaming, "I've been hit. I've been hit. Get me to a hospital. I'm dying." I yelled at him to shut up, that I was also hit. Staying low level I headed for Baldy, which is the closest base that had a medical unit.

I now have the balls to look down and I see my boot, and it looks like it is still attached to my foot and leg, so I put it back on the peddle, and got the helicopter going straight again. The wind was whistling through the holes and the helicopter was making some really strange noises. The further you are from help, the louder the noises become. I swear I could hear that little H-13 singing in my ear, "I think I can. I think I can."

As I started my decent into the medevac pad the engine finally quit and I dropped the last few feet to mother earth. Some guy ran out and started yelling that I can't park there. I told him unless he wants to get some friends to pick the -13 up and carry it, that is where it will be staying. I told him that I was wounded, but he needed to check on the major first. The major jumped out of the helicopter with his map and a marker pen and started around the front of the bubble yelling, "I am going to fix those fuckers who shot me!" At that point he passed out, and fell on his face. A couple of medics ran up with a stretcher and loaded the major, while another medic helped me into the aid tent. They cut off my boots and pants and started pulling shrapnel out of my legs and right butt cheek. I had so many pieces of metal poking out of me, I looked like a porcupine. The only protection we had in the -13 was the chicken plate we wore, and a square of armor we sat on. I must have had my ass hanging off the armor plate a little.

The medics covered me in orange antiseptic, wrapped me up in bandages, and then filled the other butt cheek with about three syringes of antibiotic and pain killers. I was told to take it easy for a couple of days, and that I would have chunks of metal coming out of my body for awhile. Very true. Twenty years later I was still picking pieces of shrapnel from various places. Most were in the legs and butt, but several migrated to my arms and back. I was also told by a giggling medic, that they had rushed the major into surgery, stripped him naked, and then didn't find a single thing wrong with him. It is funny that he got a shit pot full of medals for his actions that day, but he did not want anyone talking to me about it. I did get a Purple Heart, but that's because the medics had to do paper work on me. I was also awarded the "Green Weenie with Barbed Wire Cluster" for being a dumb shit, and getting myself shot down.

I got a ride back over to my tent and had just laid down when the 1st Cav. Catholic Chaplin, Father Pat, popped in. This character had been a marine fighter pilot in Korea and then became a priest. He never seemed to lose his Marine Corp upbringing and could fight, drink and cuss with the best of them. The first time we met was when I got to the 1st Cav. and attended Mass. We did not have a church, but were herded to a clearing on the perimeter and told that was where Mass would be held. I remember waiting with everyone else for a few minutes, when here comes this priest riding a small tote goat, motor scooter. He pulled up and parked, walked to the edge of the clearing and looked out at the jungle. He then yelled, "Charlie, don't be fucking with me right now. I have to give Mass to the boys." He then held church services right there.

Father Pat and I became friends, and would run into each other every month or so at some fire base or bar. If we were in a bar he would reach the point where he had drank enough, that he would start giving demonstrations of PLF's. I think these letters stood for Parachute Landing Falls, or whatever these dumb parachutists call them. It involves locking your legs together and bending them slightly. When you touch down you roll onto your thigh, butt and back so as to protect yourself from getting hurt. I prefer to call them PFL's (Plain Fucking Lucky) if you get to this point after jumping out of an airplane. The next thing you would know, Father Pat would be standing on top of the bar, yell and then fling himself toward the floor. He would then complete his PLF to the roar of the crowd, and be offered even more to drink.

He showed up with two cases of beer that he had "acquired" from somewhere, and the two of us sat in the tent and drank until we couldn't stand up. He then said a little prayer over me, got up, and staggered off. I stayed drunk for 2 days, and then was back flying the missions.

# GRASS AS HIGH AS AN ELEPHANTS EYE

I became a magnet for bullets and within ten days, managed to get my butt shot down three times. If you are allergic to lead, I guess it is best to avoid a war zone.

There was a lot of talk going on through the intelligence circles that a very large force of North Vietnamese soldiers were coming down out of the Que Son Valley to the west, and they were going to cut Highway 1. The Que Son was one of the most frequently used terminuses of the Ho Chi Minh trail. There were reports that at least two regiments of the 2nd NVA Division, the 3rd and the 21st, were using the valley. This put them right in my neck of the woods, and my little home would be a target for them.

A U.S infantry company was working its way toward the valley to our west, and started taking fire from everywhere. They were in danger of being surrounded and cut off. A Lt. from artillery came down and told me to wind up the -13. We had to go help the grunts. I flew us out low level and had the skids right in the tops of the trees. I didn't want to get shot down again so soon, or ever, so was doing my damnest to stay hidden. The NVA had anti aircraft capabilities and some of these were radar controlled. If they saw you and tried to track the helicopter, you would start hearing a beep-beep-beep tone in your headset. If the beeping got louder and faster, you knew they had you locked on. Talk about a way to pucker your ass and suck the cushion off the seat. I never had one ever take shots at me, but I heard the tone ringing in my headset a time or two. I saw a Huey flying past one time, with little puffs of smoke chasing him the entire way. He finally realized what was going on, and dove down into the tree tops. That made a believer out of me.

I arrived out with the infantry unit and began doing forward scouting for them, and then the Lt. started calling in artillery fire. There were enemy targets everywhere and we could hardly keep up with places to shoot, and now it was starting to get dark. I was still in the tree tops and could look straight down at the infantry. As soon as I moved out from their location, I would draw AK-47 fire from below me. They weren't hitting me, but it was only a matter of time. We were right in the mouth of the valley and every time I would come around from the east to west, NVA .51 cal. machine guns would start firing at me, trying to knock me out of the sky. These .51s were hidden in caves and could not be hit with airstrikes. If artillery was called in, they would simply roll the machine guns back inside the tunnels. I turned off all of my lights and kept flying in circles inside the valley. The NVA would listen and open up on me when they thought I was close.

U.S forces used a nice red tracer for their guns, but everything coming at me was green tracers, and they looked like great big floating basketballs as they arched up into the sky. My butt was puckered so that I kept pulling in more power and before I knew it I had that little H-13 up to about 6,000 feet. The green tracers kept going by below me, so I didn't care if I had nose bleed or not. I stayed out there until I was low on fuel, and then headed back in for the night. I was not doing the grunts any good anyway. I could not see the ground well enough to identify enemy movement. The infantry unit broke contact with the NVA, and formed a perimeter for protection. The artillery put a ring of steel around the grunts, by firing rounds all night long near their position.

The next day H.Q told me to head out alone and work the long flat area coming out of the valley and heading for Highway 1. The NVA that had engaged the infantry unit the previous day, had broke contact, and it was assumed they were heading east. It was unknown how many enemy were out there, so they sent me to find out. I was out there all by myself and there is nothing for miles in any direction, but rice fields. Now the rice isn't grass and I didn't have an elephant, but if I did and he had short legs, then it would have come up to his eye balls. At this time of year the rice hadn't been harvested and had grown about three or four feet tall. I figured I would just fly with my skids in the top of the rice and that should keep me in a nice low profile. I worked back and forth for a while, and didn't see a single, living thing. I guess I didn't remember a previous lesson learned in a little village. It was just too damn quiet. I then headed west to work more toward the mountain, and was flying so low that the rice stalks were banging into the chin bubble. I figured I would try and pick up the NVA trail from where they had last been seen.

Out of now where an NVA soldier stood up in front of the helicopter and was maybe 150 feet away. I was flying at about thirty or forty

.m.p.h and started closing on him rapidly. He brought his rifle up and aimed right at me. I saw the smoke come out of his barrel, and heard the bullet go zinging by my head. It came in right in front of my face, blew a hole in the bubble and went out through the top, hitting the rotor blades. I took some cuts to the face from the plastic shrapnel, but was otherwise uninjured. All of this happened so fast, all I could do was keep on flying toward him. As I passed him from about five feet away, he was looking at me as if to say, "How in the hell did I miss you?" I couldn't even move, let alone attack him so I headed for home. I didn't think this fellow was all alone either. I also knew he had hit the engine or rotor system with his shot, and had no idea what extent the damage was. I sure as hell didn't want to end up having to sit down out in the rice paddy by myself.

I landed and refueled, made my report and then got out a bottle of bourbon I had stashed. I sat and drank, and did not fly for the rest of the day. The helicopter had to be replaced, and sent for repairs before it could be put back into action. A replacement bird arrived a couple of days later and it was back to the war.

I was really beginning to wonder why everywhere I went someone wanted to kill me. 1st Cav. units went out to that area the next day and stumbled into a NVA battalion that was hiding on a large hill in the middle of the rice paddies. This battalion consisted of approximately 300 men, and they were dug in and ready for a fight. There were helicopters being shot down left and right, and a friend of mine who was involved in the battle, told me that his Huey got hit. They made an emergency landing in the rice paddy and got out to form a perimeter. They couldn't shut the helicopter off due to the damage, so the helicopter just sat there and ran, until it was out of fuel.

Things were really popping in our area during this time. It was a couple of days later that a scout ship put out a call, early in the morning, that he had a large NVA unit moving from the coastal area back toward the mountains. They were moving west up a stream that was near the village, where I had gotten shot. Everyone who had a gun flew out there, and we got into a large circle and started attacking the enemy. I had one of the artillery Lts. with me and he had his M-60. The gunships would make a pass and then we would fly parallel to the stream, and he would let loose with the machine gun. Then someone else would make a run, and we would start all over again. Pretty soon this little stream was running red, and there were bodies everywhere. I had never seen anything like it. The body count later was over 100 enemy dead. They were just left where they lay. I'm sure someone carried them off for burial later, but I do not know if it was us or the enemy.

We were engaging the enemy just about every day somewhere around the area of operations (AO). I had the Huey out one day for a re-supply run, and we spotted an NVA soldier running through a grave yard near a village. He was carrying a weapon so was fair game. My door gunners engaged him and he ducked behind a large head stone. The gunners had him pinned there and just kept hammering away while I circled around and around. They finally killed him, so we set down and they grabbed the weapon he had been carrying. This was an SKS rifle that still had Cosmo line on it. The gun had a folding bayonet and looked brand new. The crew chief gave me the gun, and I put it in my tent when we got back to Baldy. I was going to figure a way to send it home. I knew you couldn't send home an AK-47 because they were an automatic weapon, but figured a rifle would be okay. The next day a major came down and told me that I could not have war souvenirs and confiscated it. I'm sure it ended up in either his officers club, or he sent it home, with a great story on how he captured it.

# WE HAVE YOUR HIGH SMOKE STREAMER

1st Cav. units got involved in a large scale assault on village complexes to our east. These were on the coastal plain between Hwy 1 and the South China Sea. Everyone scrambled to the area and I was sent out with a fairly new Lt., who was assigned to the artillery. This guy was dumber than a rock, or maybe just lacked common sense, and wore glasses so thick that they looked like the bottom of a pop bottle. He was known, not so affectionately as "Mr. Magoo".

We flew east from Baldy and were soon over the fighting. Everywhere I looked there were helicopter gunships making firing runs, and troop ships dropping the infantry in blocking positions. I got over the village area and was making tight circles to the left and looking straight down from about fifty feet. This was really flat ground and had enormously tall palm trees everywhere. As I looked straight down, I could see the pathways between the village huts. On every path there were enemy troops running this way and that.

The NVA soldiers, wearing their tan uniforms and carrying AK-47s, were running everywhere, so I told the Lt. to get ready to engage them. He had an M-60 sticking out the door so I rolled into a tight right turn. I told him, "Start shooting everyone down there in light brown and wearing a pith helmet."
He kept saying, "I can't see anyone. Where are they?"
I kept yelling at him, "Open fire."

I figured that if he would just shoot straight down I could dance the H-13 around and make the bullets go where they were intended. But he just wouldn't fire. I called two gunships up, and told them about the enemy I had below me. They responded that they would form up behind me and engage. I told them I would get over the NVA again, and drop a smoke grenade straight down. I told Magoo to get ready to drop the grenade, and he reached over and grabbed something from my box and pulled the pin. Before I could stop him, he flung a quick fuse, white phosphorus grenade out his side. The quick fuses were set to go off in three seconds, and he had already used up about one and a half seconds, after he pulled the pin. This grenade went off a little below and behind the engine compartment, near the tail boom. The gunships called and were laughing their ass off. I heard them saying, "War Eagle. War Eagle. We have your high smoke streamer." Then they fell into another fit of laughter.

In artillery fire when you want to make sure that your rounds are going where they are intended, you have the artillery fire a smoke round for identification purposes. As it descends it trails smoke hence the name high smoke streamer. They came in Red, Yellow, and Purple, but were sometimes white. Today it was white. I now have a helicopter that may or may not be on fire, so off I went back to the base as fast as that little bird could go. When I landed I found that a lot of paint on the tail boom had been singed off. The helicopter was still able to fly, but I wasn't going anywhere with this blind guy. I told the command post to either get me a different Lt. or I wasn't flying. There were no one left so I sat out the rest of that battle.

185

**WEDDING DAY**

**PUTTING THE BARBERING SKILLS TO WORK**

**GRADUATION FROM FLIGHT SCHOOL**

## MY USUAL VIEW OF VIETNAM

**Ft. HOOD TX**

# LANE ARMY AIRFIELD

# BY THE SEAT OF MY PANTS

The entire South China Sea area, which included South and North Vietnam, and China got hit with a typhoon. I had never been hit with a hurricane, and had no idea what to expect from a typhoon, which is the southern hemisphere equivalent. We lashed down everything that might get blown away, and piled more sandbags around the helicopters and tents. It rained and rained and rained some more, while the wind blew. All the water was going sideways and you couldn't keep anything dry, so why bother. All flight operations except for emergencies were cancelled.

When the storm finally subsided after a couple of days we found we were completely surrounded by water. LZ Baldy was on a hill near Hwy 1, and we were a few miles inland of the South China Sea. However, now the sea had come to visit and turned us into an island. The only way in or out was by helicopter, so everyone who flew was busy hauling commanders out to visit their troops in the field. For the next few days I became a taxi, shuttling people to and from their various units. All the brass insisted they had priority, but we just took them as they came.

I got a message from LZ Two Bits that I needed to bring my helicopter down there for its scheduled maintenance. This was a minor over haul of the helicopter, and they check it from top to bottom to make sure the squirrel hasn't died, and the thing will fly. The crew chief always goes with the helicopter, so I told him to pack his stuff. We would leave in the morning to fly back to Two Bits, which was 60-70 miles south of Baldy. The next morning looked iffy from a weather standpoint. The clouds were down really low, but then I was use to flying in the tree tops, so this didn't bother me. I took off at about 7:00 a.m. and headed east toward the sea. I figured at least there I wouldn't fly into anything. As the saying goes, *"There are old pilots and there are bold pilots, but there are no, old bold pilots."* This little ditty meant don't take chances as the laws of the universe would catch up and kill you. As I flew east I ran smack into a fog bank, and I was enveloped immediately. I could not see a damn thing except for white cotton candy, up, down and to the sides. Talk about enough pucker factor to suck the seat cushion again. I was above the village area where all the fighting was still going on, so sitting down there was not an option. Turning around wouldn't work, because I had absolutely no way of finding Baldy in this soup. I knew there were trees and mountains behind me, and I knew there was beach and sea in front of me. What I did was slow down so that I was barely moving forward, and lowered down until I could make out trees.

I went east following my compass until the trees disappeared. I then knew I was on the coast or over the sea. I had the crew chief unbuckle his harness and lay on the floor, with his head hanging out. His feet were under my legs and hanging out the other side. I then let down until I could make out the waves breaking on the beach. Not knowing who was where, or if we were in the middle of enemy territory, I could not just land on the beach and wait it out. I had no desire to end up walking to North Vietnam, and spending the rest of my life in the

Hanoi Hilton. So with the crew chief looking down, I flew very slowly south down the beach. Every time I would see a dark shape in front, I would slow to a walk and edge up. These were usually large rocks dotting the coast. I would then go out to sea and around them, and then edge back into the beach to continue our trek. By watching my map I knew how many rivers I would have to come upon, until I found the Song Lai River, which flowed out of the valley to the west of Two Bits. I finally found the Song Lai and turned west. In from the coast was Hwy 1 and the bridge over this had been blown up years before. A right turn at the bridge and a short flight north put me right into LZ Two Bits. Piece of cake.

I could not even begin to describe how scary that trip was, but I never admitted it to anyone. The crew chief thought I knew exactly what I was doing the entire time, and being a daunting Army Aviator, I sure as hell wasn't going to change his image of me. There would be stories around the camp fire tonight. I'll bet I sweated 10 pounds off of my already slim frame and of course needed another trip to the bar. It's amazing how good bourbon will dull the heeby jeebies. Pretty soon you say to yourself, "Well that really wasn't too bad. I am an invincible Army Aviator, and I can do anything." And you go fly again.

# NAVY WINGS

One of my other missions was to provide fire support for the Navy.
They would sail up and down the coast, and usually fire their big guns
in support of the Marines. During my time, I fired the guns for the
Battleship New Jersey, which had been reactivated. With all Navy
gunfire I found one truism. I don't think I ever saw them hit South
Vietnam. They would have a target area identified by grid coordinates
and that is where they said they were shooting. However I would be
out there flying around their target area and never see anything hit the
ground. I mean the New Jersey is shooting bullets the size of a
Volkswagen. You should be able to see the ground go boom, or some
trees flying in the air. Nope! Nothing.

I got a call one day to fly to LZ English, which was just north of Two
Bits, and pick up a passenger from the Navy. When I landed, a
Destroyer skipper was there, and I got out and we shook hands. He
told me that his ship was currently sailing up and down our section of
the coast, and he wanted to see what happened when they fired at
targets inland. I got tuned into their fire control center on the ship, and
we flew out to the coast. The ship was sailing maybe a half mile from
the beach, and was in an area that had numerous caves in the rocks.
We were going to adjust fire for the destroyer and see if we could hit
the caves, and the skipper was along to see how well his ship did.

We spent the next hour or so shooting at the caves. These were located on the face of a cliff formation, which looked east above the South China Sea. The entire hill side was two or three hundred feet high, and at the bottom were rocks sticking out of the water. I did not want to get too close to the cave entrances, and find myself looking into the barrel of a .51 caliber machine gun. That would ruin a perfectly good day, up to that point. I did buzz the cliff face only allowing a few quick seconds in front of any of the openings. I have said before, the Navy seemed to have a problem with accuracy. About every other round that was fired, the ships commander would look at me and then ask, "Any idea where that one went?" We finally finished up and I asked the skipper where he wanted to be dropped off. He pointed east out to sea, and said he wanted to go to his boat. No one had told me shit about this plan, and I had no life vests or flotation devises. I discovered earlier in a lake, these little old helicopter just didn't do well floating. Being an intrepid aviator, and not wanting the Navy to have any reason to doubt my abilities, I turned east and headed out to sea. *"Just sit right back and you'll hear a tale. A tale of a fateful trip, that started from this Tropic port, aboard this time ship."*

Meanwhile, the ship had also turned east and was now a couple of miles off shore. I headed in that direction, the whole time waiting for a little cough or hiccup from the engine. The farther out to sea I go, the more strange noises I began to hear. I finally came to a hover over the fantail of the destroyer, and all I could see was this little tiny deck on the back of the boat. The ship had anti- submarine capabilities and had this small helicopter, which they could launch. The deck they used was maybe eight feet by eight feet, but looked a lot smaller from where I was sitting. I confirmed with the captain that this was where he wanted me to land, and I started my first approach. Meanwhile the destroyer has moved even further out to sea and is now going up and down with the swells, and at the same time going forward. I would come in over that little deck and try to stop and set down. As soon as I came to a hover I would begin mimicking the ship going up and down so now I look like a yo-yo, and I was getting sea sick. I tried three times to set down, and just could not get the hang of it. Finally I asked the Skipper for the radio frequency for the ship's bridge, so I could talk to them. I dialed it up and contacted the bridge, and told them I was coming in one more time. What I wanted was several strong sailors and some chain. When I got over that tiny deck, I was going to cut power and just drop down. When I hit I wanted the crew to grab me and then chain the -13 to the deck. In retrospect this sounds really stupid, but in reality it worked like a charm, and the U.S Navy was suitably impressed with my flying skills.

I shut down and the Skipper unloaded, and then I was given a VIP tour of the ship. As I made my way around I was provided with real food from their mess hall. I mean all I have eaten in months is either C-rations or re-constituted B-rations. Nothing like powered milk, eggs, potatoes etc for a boy to want his mothers cooking. The guys on the ship even gave me ice cold milk. I'm lactose intolerant and could not have cared if it made me crap my pants. I was drinking it. When we got all done they gave me a case of steaks and a lighter with the ships name and emblem, and we then went topside to say good bye. I got up there after having been in the bowels of the ship, and it was pitch ass black. I mean there are no lights anywhere. The Skipper told me we were about five miles out from the coast and of course I asked, "And just where that would be?" They pointed. I told them I was going to crank up and turn on every light I owned. "When I head out please watch the lights, and if for some reason the lights disappear, come and haul me out of the water."

I lifted off and headed for dry land with all these thoughts going through my head about sharks, and sea snakes. I never was so glad to be back over Vietnam, where they were only waiting to shoot at me. At least I wouldn't be eaten.

# AIR FORCE ASSHOLES

South of Two Bits was the American Air Force Base, Phu Cat, where a lot of the fighters and bombers were stationed. Talk about a different world. They lived in air conditioned brick buildings and had all the amenities of a state side AFB. You could get ice cream on your way back from the movies. How about a burger and fries after a strenuous game of tennis? I got sent down to Phu Cat on some kind of ass and trash mission, and I guess I was just a little jealous. When I departed for home I flew a little too close to the tennis courts, and sort of blew dust and debris all over the air force guys, in their pretty little tighty whities. I left north bound to one fingered salutes.

A few days later several of us were lying around the tent in the late afternoon, when Armageddon arrived. There was this god awful noise that just about blew out my ear drums, followed by part of the tent collapsing. We thought we had been hit by an enemy bomb, but knew the V.C didn't have any air planes. As I crawled out of the tent, I discovered that two air force jets had made a low level pass over the top of our home, and were last seen screaming toward the mountains to the west. I later talked to the guys in the airfield tower and found out that the two fighters were from Phu Cat AFB. They had requested a low level flyby of LZ Two Bits. *"Hi there Two Bits. We would like to perform a small air show for the benefit of "War Eagle". Can you tell us where he lives?"* They came streaking in and when they got over our area they went vertical and into after burner. Once past Two Bits they dropped back down to low level over the paddies and skedaddled.

Somehow the air force did some Intel and found out where I lived, and decided to pay me a visit. I never went anywhere near Phu Cat again, and believed that next time they might, just drop a bomb on me.

# BANG COCK

I got called in to the commander's tent and was told that I would be heading back up to Baldy, as that was where all the action was going on. I was also asked if I wanted to go to Thailand on a five day R & R first. The pilot who was supposed to go, got himself shot and couldn't make it. "Let me think about that for a half second. Hell yes!" and ran to pack. I had maybe two items of civilian clothing left from my trip to Hawaii, and borrowed clothes from the rest of the guys.

I left with a small suitcase and about $100 in my pocket. When I arrived in Bangkok I picked a clean, but really cheap hotel and paid for the five days in advance. I figured I would find a way to eat and shop on what was left. Bangkok was very inexpensive at this time. The first thing I did was apply for a sponsorship program from the embassy. They hooked me up with a military person stationed there, and his job was to take me on some guided tours and basically take care of me. I had an old time sergeant, who took me under his wing and drove me to all the sights. He took me to see the floating market, and several of the really ornate temples that dot the city. The next day we got into his jeep and drove out of the city and into the jungle to the north. After spending most of my time above the trees and getting shot at, it was really pleasant to spend time just looking at how beautiful everything was. For some reason I was also a little nervous. I kept looking for little brown men with guns, behind the trees.

I got some advance pay from the military payroll office at the embassy to tide me over. Then the Sgt. and I headed out to do some shopping. The two of us ended up down in the main, market district. I wandered into a jewelry shop and started looking around. The Sgt. took about fifteen seconds to become bored, and then gave me direction to my hotel, so when I finished up I could walk back. My hotel was no more than a half mile from where I was standing.

I was looking at rings for Heleen and wanted to buy something really nice, but knew I had to be careful as I did not have much money. I was looking at Fire Opals when this Thai about my age, introduced himself as Mr. David and told me he was the owner of the store. He asked who I was and where I was from, and why I was looking at rings. It didn't take long for him to understand that I wanted an inexpensive ring and why. When I finished that day I had a beautiful Fire Opal ring and a black Star Safire ring, and had paid about $50 for both. Mr. D told me later that he owned a silk factory and a gem mine plus the jewelry store. The guy was very rich, but was down to earth and extremely nice.

Mr. David asked if I had plans for that night and I informed him that I was just going to hang out at the hotel and watch TV. The hotel had a bar, and like every other hotel in Thailand, it had its own stable of hookers. They would sit in the bar until employed, and I would sit with them and drink Singha beer and chit chat in pigeon English. It was either sit in the bar or sit in my room. The only thing on T.V was Thai kick boxing. I couldn't understand a word and didn't know what was going on, so that became boring real quick. It got to the point where the girls knew I was married but broke, and a couple of them offered me a freebee, if I was so inclined. These girls were hookers because they were not pure Thai. The only job open to them was as escorts and prostitutes. They were a mixture of Thai and Indian, and were absolutely beautiful.

Mr. David said he was going to come by and pick me up later and I was to be his guest that night for dinner and a tour of Bangkok. I met Mr. D in the lobby about 6:00 p.m. and the two of us got into his car. We went to an exclusive club that was members only and consisted mostly of rich Thai and Chinese, and a few Americans. When I entered I passed by this large glassed- in room with stadium style seating. On the seats were Thai girls, all wearing the same kimonos type uniform, with numbers on them. I think there were about 100 girls, but they all looked alike to me. It reminded me of a display case in a grocery store. *"O.K. I'll take one of these and two of those. Don't bother to wrap them".*

We went into the bar, which was breathtaking. One whole rear wall was a waterfall about fifteen feet tall. We had cocktails and some snacks, then Mr. D said we were going to have a massage before we went out to dinner. He took me back to the window, where I was to select my masseuse. They all looked the same, so I just picked a number and told him that was my choice. They notified the girl and one that Mr. D had picked, and they met us on the stairway going up. Right away these two girls started jabbering back and forth like crazy, and looking at me. Mr. D told me that neither had ever given a massage to a white man before, and they were not sure if this was going to work out. Mine didn't speak a word of English, so I wasn't so sure how this would work out either. I had not learned the universal sign language for, "Happy ending" yet.

We ended up in small rooms upstairs, that consisted of a large bathtub and a massage table. My girl filled the bathtub with hot water and then informed me to get undressed, put on a robe and then when she left, for me to get into the tub. All of this was done via pantomime and Mr. D yelling from down the hall. I had been in Thailand for two full days, and had taken probably four or five showers in the hotel. I got into the tub, and the water turned black. The girl came back into the room, took one look at water, and started yelling at the top of her lungs. Pretty soon Mr. D's girl is in my room and both are pointing at the water and yelling. Then Mr. D arrived and told me that the girls think I'm some kind of Neanderthal, because I'm so dirty. I explain to him about being in the jungle most of the time, with no showers and that the dirt must be just ground in. I now have to get out of the bathtub while they drain, and then refill it, and this procedure was repeated two more times before the water stayed clear. After finally getting clean it was back out of the tub and unto the table for a wonderful massage. I slept through most of it.

When we finished Mr. D and I went out to a Thai night club for dinner and drinks. After we had eaten and watched a stage show for a while he said we were going back to his club for another massage, but no bath. He said all the rich Thai do this and I could see where it would be addicting. I picked the same girl I had before rather than go through the entire rigmarole I had been through earlier. This massage was a shortened version of the one before dinner, and I was now ready for bed.

Mr. D and I went down stairs and as we were leaving, he asked me to wait a minute while he went back into the club. When he came back out he said everything was all arranged, and the girl that had given me my massages would come to the hotel and live with me until I left for Vietnam. I told Mr. D that I appreciated all his hospitality and everything he had done for me, but that I was married and would have to decline. Two days later I was back living in a tent. Everyone is telling me that either I am a liar, or an idiot, depending on whether they believe my story or not.

# CHU LAI AND BALDY

I was back up north and things were still popping out in the boonies. I was flying continually it seemed. It felt like that H-13 was welded to my ass. It was not so much that I was in the air continually, but I was always with my bird. Fly here. Shut down and wait. Fly there. Pick someone up and fly somewhere else where he confers with someone. Go visit an artillery unit, and then go out and assist the grunts by flying re-con and firing the big guns for them. I would be gone from 6:00 a.m. to 6:00 p.m. and only have four actual hours in the air. Other days I might have 12 hours airborne. It was best summed up as, "Hours and hours of boredom, interrupted by a few moments of pure terror."

I was sitting on a small fire base way out in the mountains west of Baldy, when the ground just started dancing. There was a B-52 Arc Light mission going in a little west of where I was sitting, and I could see the shock waves coming toward me, and rippling across the tree tops. The -52s were carpet bombing the mountains and trails the NVA were using. The B-52s carried up to 108 bombs in their belly, and another 24 bombs on the wings. I couldn't see them, but there were as many as twenty or thirty planes on that mission. The only way to describe the feeling, is that it similar to being compressed and then expanded, over and over. My heart was doing strange things, and felt like it would pop out of my chest.

After the Arc Light I was sitting and waiting on my passenger, when an infantryman wandered by. He stopped and looked at me then said, "You pilots have it made. Flying around in that armor plated helicopter with that bullet proof bubble."

I replied, "If you look closely you can see where the bullets went through this nice, bullet proof bubble. See where the crew chief has wired the holes shut, with safety wire". Then I pointed out the little piece of armor plating I sit on.

The last I heard from him was, "Maybe I will just stay here on the ground".

I started doing bombing missions just to have something else at my disposal for screwing with the enemy. I found some mason jars down in the village market. I pulled the pin on a hand grenade, and then slid the grenade into the jar. The handle that flies off when you throw the grenade, stays in place until you drop the bomb, and the jar breaks. The handle flies off and the grenade arms, and a few seconds later; Boom! Any altitude works, because the bomb won't go off until the glass jar hits the ground. Actually this was just a silly diversion, and I don't think I ever found a suitable target. I eventually ran out of mason jars anyway.

I had to go to Chu Lai AFB for some minor maintenance on my bird, lifted off Baldy and headed south down Hwy 1. It was about a one hour trip in the -13 and I was cruising along at 1500 feet and maybe doing 60 m.p.h. I heard this god awful racket, and I couldn't identify it. It sounded like I had just been dropped in the middle of the Indy

500.

I looked around and found an A1E fighter, flying formation off my left rear. The A1E had been around the Air force forever and was a prop driven fighter bomber. They were very effective at close air support, because they could carry a lot of bombs and bullets, and could stay on station over a battle for a long time. They were also used in the rescue of downed pilots in North Vietnam, Laos, and Cambodia areas. They were famous and known by their call sign: "Sandy". This one flying to my left, had his wheels down and flaps fully extended, so that he could slow way down to meet my speed. I was staring at him and he's waving at me, and grinning like he's in some kind of parade. He then pointed to his right and indicated that I should look. I leaned forward and twisted my head, and there is his wingman flying off my right rear. The wingman is also waving like an idiot, and the two of them now have a great story about flying formation with the slowest helicopter, operating in Vietnam. After a few minutes of this they "clean up" their planes by pulling the wheels back up and raising their flaps, and then roar by me, while climbing. When last seen they were heading south toward Chu Lai. I was sure that in about an hour they will be in the O' club telling everyone how they made my day.

I was feeling pretty cool having just been the lead for a flight of three. I was getting closer to Chu Lai so I gave their tower a call to tell them I was north of the field for landing. They were familiar with my call sign "War Eagle 69" and I expected a snappy reply from them with directions. I think they may have already had a conversation with the two A1Es, so the tower operator came back with: "Understand War Eagle is five miles north for landing. Please call back tomorrow when you get closer." This was followed by laughter from every airplane within range. The Air Force pukes just loved sticking it to us lowly helicopter pilots. I think it was jealousy because they had to read maps and instruments to get from point A to B, while a helicopter pilot could come to a hover, and read the road signs or the name on the water tower.

We did get payback on the Air Force on occasion and when we did it was very, very sweet. I remember a day when we first arrived at Chu Lai as a group. I think there were four helicopters and pilots, and we had just parked near the taxi way. Our unit did not have a home yet so we had to wait for a place to park permanently. We were standing around smoking and joking while all these jets were taking off and landing. Chu Lai was located right on the South China Sea, so there was sand everywhere. The helicopters really stirred up a dust storm whenever we had to lift off or land, and the Air Force wasn't our biggest fan.

We were standing there when two F-4 Phantom jets landed and rolled out. They then turned down the taxi way to go by us. The first one passed and gave us a smirk. They had their canopies open so they can cool down and catch a breeze, but the real reason was so they can hang their arm out and say, "Whoo. Whoo. Look at me." The second Phantom got close and this shit head was wearing a scarf and thinking he's god's gift to aviation, when he ran off the taxi way and got his nose wheel stuck in the sand. He goosed his jets trying to get back on the pavement, but only succeeded in getting the plane buried deeper. We were laughing like crazy and pointing at him and making rude gestures, when he closed the canopy. Then he had to sit there cooking in the sun and wait for a tow vehicle to rescue him.

# GOOKS IN THE WIRE

It was the middle of the night and a small artillery base just south of us, was being hit by the NVA. This was a small fire base sitting in the middle of the rice paddies, out in no man's land. On the base is one battery of 105 mm canons. This consisted of about 6 or 7 guns and about 100 men. They also had a platoon of infantry assigned for perimeter security.

The first reports were that the enemy was lobbing in mortars and rockets, and a lot of small arms fire. We then got the report that the NVA had launched a ground assault against the fire base, and they estimate over 300 attackers. Everyone who could fly scrambled and there is so much gun fire and helicopter traffic that I stayed out from the fire base so as not to get run over. My H-13 gunship with the fixed site M-16, wasn't going to be much help anyway.

E/82nd has a support Huey assigned and, it was hovering over the concertina wire, while the crew chiefs were firing down into the mass of enemy with their M-60s. The Huey was trying to drop off more small arms ammunition for the troops, who were using theirs up at an alarming rate. The helicopter was piloted by Dooley and I remember the crew chief was a Hawaiian named Furtado. Dooley told me later, that Furtado was standing on the skid of the helicopter and firing continually straight down. This was happening while they were coming into the LZ low level, to kick out cases of bullets. On a mission like this you did not slow down. You would do a fly bye, and try to hit the drop point on your way past. All this while there are tracers going everywhere, and a whole lot of people trying to kill you. Ballsy stuff.

I headed back to Baldy to pick up an artillery officer so that big guns from other fire bases could be brought into the fight and then I returned to the scene of the battle. We flew around and directed artillery fire at the areas where the enemy was approaching from,, and tried to get the rounds as close to the perimeter as we could.

As the sun started coming up the NVA disengaged and were heading back for the mountains with helicopter gunships chasing them. I landed at the LZ and was told by my passenger to sit with the engine running, while he went into the camp to talk to the commander.

I was sitting outside the perimeter wire pointing west, and I had the -13 sitting at a fast idle. To my right front are two grunts that have a recoilless rifle set up and as I watched they were loading a round into the breach. All of sudden there is an explosion at the rifle, and something goes flying by the bubble in front of me. My first thought is an enemy mortar or rocket has landed, and my next thought is to get the hell out of Dodge as I'm being targeted. I pulled pitch with everything I had, and leapt off the ground and into the air. I made a couple of circles over the LZ when I was signaled to come back in and land.

I sat down near where I was before and noticed a lot of activity by the recoilless rifle. I was told to shut down by my passenger and when I did, I was informed that the soldier behind the rifle forgot to lock the breech. When he pulled the firing rope the breach flew open, and that, coupled with the exploding gases, blew his head off. That was what had flown past my bubble, and the head was still sitting in the dirt with a helmet strapped on. A human head is held on mainly be gravity. There are just a bunch of tendons and skin basically holding the noggin to the rest of the body. A good blast of pressure and gas will pull it right off the torso.

I walked into the LZ and went over to talk to the commander of the artillery unit. The guy was an absolute wreck. He was standing there shaking like a leaf and stuttering, when he tried to explain what had taken place. He said at one time he was in his fighting trench and an NVA jumped in with him. He fired every round he had in his .45 pistol but the enemy would bounce back up and come at him again. He loaded another magazine and kept shooting the guy. After two complete magazines of .45 rounds, the enemy soldier finally stayed down. That was fourteen slugs from the commander's gun. They later found that the NVA had wrapped their bodies in layers of tight bandages, so that the trauma of getting shot wouldn't put them down. Japanese soldiers in WWII did the same thing. There were also stories that the NVA were drugged up, but I don't know that to be true. They had to be smoking dope, sniffing glue or drinking Wild Turkey, to attack like that.

The commander took us on a tour and told us what had happened during the assault. The artillery unit was firing with everything it had and the perimeter guards and infantry were fighting hand to hand with the NVA. There were approximately 100 troops inside the wire and probably three times that many enemy soldiers. The artillery units have what is called a bee hive round for final self defense. This is a 105mm round filled with metal darts (flechette). It is similar to a giant shot gun shell with finned nails instead of B.Bs. When being overrun the commander would order the bee hive round. The guns would load and depress their barrels, so that they were firing at waist high level. These darts shredded the enemy and sometimes would nail the bodies together. Everywhere we walked there were pieces of enemy soldiers. I remember looking at the concertina wire and seeing an ear pinned to a barb.

Sure makes me glad that I'm a pilot and not sitting in some little LZ waiting for the enemy to show up. *Oh! It seems like I spend all of my nights doing just that.*

# I'M DONE

It's getting close to Christmas and I have less than twenty days left on this tour, before I can go home. Everyone in Vietnam has a short timer's calendar and I have been marking mine off religiously. You never start a calendar before you have 180 days left in country, and most don't start theirs until they are down to 90 days. In retrospect it is stupid. You just start learning how to fight and stay alive when all of sudden you are marking days off until you return to the USA. You are not worth a damn the first thirty days you are in Viet Nam. You spend all your time learning to stay alive. Then you get to the last 30 days, and you spend all of your time trying to remain alive. So you start doing everything to make sure you make it. You find reasons to avoid certain areas or missions. No sense in taking chances, is there?

*"War Eagle 69. War Eagle 69. This is Redman 6. Your location please."*

*"Yeah, Red Man. I'm right above you."*

*"War Eagle. I don't see you."*

*"Red Man. Look straight up. See that speck at 5,000 feet that looks like it's getting smaller? That would be me."*

A couple of us were sitting around the tent having some beers when we decided what we really needed was some Christmas spirit. Randy Bell, Ron Pincock and I, borrowed a jeep and just as its getting toward dusk we headed out for the nearest Christmas tree farm. Now they didn't really have any of these, but we were not to be deterred. Especially since we have partaken of some "Yule Tide Noggin". I'm not saying we were drunk, but we obviously were lacking in good common sense. We headed for the village of Bon Son, but turned right and headed up a nearby hill. We soon found a likely tree, pulled it out of the ground, and stuck it in the back of the jeep. On our way back we were still imbibing of the noggin and Pincock, who was driving, made a wrong turn. Now we were sitting in the middle of a rice paddy, stuck, and we are in Indian country. I got out and waded to the road.

Finally an army truck came by, and pulled us out of the mud. We got back to our air field only to be met by the M.Ps, who thought we were both idiots and drunks, but since we made it out and back without being shot by the V.C., they let us go. We got back to our tent and stuck the tree in a bucket, and then we hung some beer cans and other crap on it, and went to bed. God protects drunks and teen age pilots.

Christmas Eve arrived and we were on a "Christmas Truce" with the enemy. I don't know who makes this up, but I wonder. Did someone drive out to a rice paddy somewhere to meet in secret with the V.C., and they mutually agreed not to shoot each other for a few days? Just how did they arrange a truce? Go to a phone booth and call the other side up? I don't think so. The brass just makes this shit up, so you can go a couple of days thinking, maybe you won't be shot.

It was Christmas Eve and we were all sitting around the tent playing poker and drinking beer. Pincock had gotten a set of jungle fatigues from the supply Sgt. and found the flight line, paint locker mysteriously unlocked. He helped himself to a can and brush and proceeded to make a red Santa Clause suit for Bell. The fatigues were a little large, but Randy fit into them nicely. He then proceeded to pass out Christmas presents to everyone. No one bought a thing for the festivities, but gaily wrapped whatever was available. "Let's see. How about a can of Ham and Lima beans for Jim. I have a bar of soap, slightly used, for Francisco. Dooley! Come here and get your new can of lighter fluid for the old Chu Lai Zippo. Here is a step stool for Lazares. He's such a short timer, he can't get into his helicopter. Lastly, here is a double armored flak jacket, and preparation H for Harry."

A helicopter appeared over head being pulled by eight tiny reindeer, and began circling the LZ while blaring Christmas carols. They were using a Psy/Ops bird which had four giant speakers hanging out the sides. The Psychological Operations people were usually broadcasting messages to the enemy to give themselves up. We would build them a Wal-Mart, and give them a farm and a water buffalo. They also dropped leaflets urging the VC and NVA to quit fighting and change sides. These made great wall coverings and toilet paper.

This night they had Christmas carols. Some of the G.I.s thought this was really neat, and you could hear singing coming from some of the tents. But some of the troops are just a little bit the other side of hum bug. As the helicopter made its passes around and around the LZ, they start drawing small arms fire from some of the units. Most of it was tracer rounds sent in their general direction. I don't think anyone was crazy enough to actually think about shooting down one of our own helicopters, but you never know. I have a friend, Sunny, who was on that bird that night. He claims that he could have reached out the door and touched the bullets coming at them from Two Bits .The Psy/Ops bird decided it had better depart for friendlier skies. I guess not everyone was in the Christmas spirit.

A week later I had orders sending me home and on January 7, 1968 I was back in the good old U.S of A.

# TEXAS

I had just landed at McChord AFB and cleared customs. There were horror stories before we left the war about people getting caught trying to bring prohibited items into the U.S.A. I got into the inspection line but they took one look at my officer rank, and waved me through. I guess I should have packed that rocket launcher after all.

It was a long ass flight from Vietnam, but I was so glad to be back in the U.S. I gathered up all my baggage and found a cab outside the base ops building. Heleen was living in a trailer we had bought before I left for my tour of duty, and it was located about two miles from the base. It still seemed like a really long ride. I got out of the cab and knocked on the door. Pretty soon Heleen is staring out the window at me but is making no motion to let me in. Seems she doesn't recognize the skinny guy with the mustache, standing on her porch. I was probably weighing in somewhere in the neighborhood of 140 pounds and 10 of those was the new facial hair. Real combat aviators all had handlebar mustaches, even it meant spending twelve months trying to make it grow.

I was finally let in for my long awaited homecoming. First things first though. I needed to see and hold my daughter Michelle, who I had never met. She was now eight months old and was the cutest thing I had ever seen. She took one look at this new face and started crying. But it didn't take us long to become best friends.

I had to report to Fort Hood, Texas in about thirty days, so everything was hectic with the packing and getting the trailer ready to go. Family and friends put a lot of demands on my time. "Come on over. I want to see where you got shot. Did you get to kill anyone? What did it feel like?" All the questions I did not want to answer.

Everyone wanted to see me, or have me over for dinner or a party. The last thing I wanted to do was stand around and tell war stories. I remember one really embarrassing moment at my aunt's place. She threw a party for me and there must have been a couple of dozen relatives and friends in the house. A bunch of us were standing in the kitchen area and the group spilled over into the laundry room. The bar had been set up on top of the washing machine. The dryer was sitting next to the washer and the dryer door was partially open. Someone pushed the door shut, and the dryer started up with a loud bang. Everyone was now staring at me, as I lay on the laundry room floor in a fetal position with my arms over my head. They all thought it was hilarious, but I couldn't stop shaking, and my heart was going about 100 miles a minute.

Heleen and I finally finished packing and the trailer was ready to head to Texas. We were going to caravan down with the truck pulling our trailer, but that plan went to hell in Oregon. The driver had been fighting with his wife, and she poured sugar into his gas tank. The truck got towed into a service station, and we were told it would take about three or four days to get it back running. So we left everything by the side of the road and Heleen, Michelle and I continued our drive to Texas.

The town of Killeen was garden spot of Texas. Besides Ft. Hood, its claim to fame is having a home owned by Elvis Presley, who had been stationed there in 1958. Some people are just better than others, and do not have to live in the drafty old WWII buildings. We had already made arrangements to have the trailer parked in a small court in town, but until it arrived we were living in the Ft. Hood Inn. This was a hotel for military personnel but this one was pretty much a dump. This building was erected during WW II and hasn't been renovated recently. All of the rooms are small and not richly appointed. Plus there is not a lot of insulation between rooms, so you can listen all night to the couple down the hall, either fighting or fornicating. We were very glad it was short term.

I reported to the 2nd Armored Division Headquarters to find out what my new assignment would be. I was informed that I would not be signing in and that I was to be thrown out of the Army. Seems that a certain captain had managed to file the same report that he submitted to Colonel Putnam only this time he did it behind the back of the 1st Cav. I explained to the Chief of Staff for the Division everything that had transpired. He told me to go home and take a couple of days to settle in, and he would call me. Two days later I got a call from the Division G-1, which handled personnel. Right away I knew things were right in my world because he's a colonel and I'm a warrant officer, and he's calling me, "Sir. "Yes Sir, Mr. Lazares. If it's convenient for you, could you drop by the Division. You can come in today or tomorrow. It's entirely up to you. Thank you, Sir."

I went into the post and met with the G-1, who informs me that General Tolson, the Commanding Officer of the 1st Cav. had been contacted and confirmed all the information I had provided. Gen. Tolson followed this up by informing the 2nd A.D. that he was personally sending a Special Officer Efficiency Report, on me, to them and would follow up with another phone call. He made it clear that I was to be extended every courtesy.

I signed in to the post and learned I'll be assigned to a Cav. unit. I'm excited until I learn it's an Armored Cav., and they don't seem to have helicopters. Plus, even if they did, I'm the only pilot in the unit. I went over there and they had no clue as to what to do with me. They assigned me a bunch of duties so that I stayed out of the way. I was the only combat veteran in the unit and the only warrant officer, and all these baby lieutenants just don't know what to make of me. The Cav. unit is their training ground after basic officer training, and they need to learn to drive tanks and armored personnel carriers. What do they know about helicopter integration?

A couple of weeks later I was informed that we would be having a unit formation and I will be getting some of the medals I had been awarded in Vietnam. The whole unit lined up on the parade ground. I was standing out front and the commander pinned on the Purple Heart, a couple of Bronze Stars, and an Air Medal with about a dozen oak leaf clusters. I've gone from being the unit oddity to a celebrity. What drove the army mentality then as well as now, was for the soldiers to go to battle and earn medals. It remains one of the biggest benchmarks of a man's self worth. Most of these officers cannot wait to get out of Ft. Hood and get to combat, and I wish there was some way that I could convince them that it ain't nearly as cool as they think.

One bright spot in the unit was this dippy 2nd Lt. named "C" which was short for clueless. But his real claim to fame was he was married to a girl who had been a playboy fold out in the 60's. She was short, with dark hair and probably the biggest set of boobs I had ever seen. Rumor had it that when they were living at another army post, while he went through Officer Candidate School, she was entertaining all the males in the apartment building. The story went that one day Lt. C left for class, and got about half way there when he discovered he had forgotten his hat. He returned only to find Miss Chesty in bed with a couple of the neighbors. He forgave her because of her obvious attributes, but was keeping a real close eye on her. I was on his side, so I kept a real close eye on her also.

We would have a unit Officers Call and they would show up. Mrs. C always wore dresses that showed everything from her nose to her navel, and she always had a crowd around her. I remember one night we were at the colonels' and everyone was drinking and smoking. We were standing around a coffee table where the ashtray was, and every time she bent over to flick her ashes, the general, the colonel, a couple of Lt. colonels and a few others, would all start to bend over unconsciously to peer down her dress. It reminded me of the bobble head bird. You would tip his beak into a glass of water and let him go. His head would then bob up and down until you stopped him. It wasn't long before some of the wives gathered up their distracted bobble heads and headed home. A few months later Mrs. C met up with another Lt's wife, who also had a reputation for being a stray, and the two of them let out for California to make their fame and fortune. They probably ended up starring in some porn flicks, but I wouldn't know. I don't think I could recognize her face.

# BACK IN THE CAVALRY

We had set up home in our little trailer and were busy making new friends in the neighborhood. I had four, single lieutenants living in a house next door, so they got adopted. Heleen found a young girl with two kids, living down the street. Her husband was in Nam, so she got adopted. All of the single aviators became part of the family. That was Army life. Everyone took care of each other.

The Cav. just is not my cup of tea so I began hanging out at the 2nd Armored Division flight detachment, located at the base airfield. But the Cav. still owns me, and they have decided they want to go on a training exercise out in the desert. It was still winter and colder than I am used to, but they want me along as the scout helicopter for the unit's movement. I would be living in a tent for a week and I was not a happy camper. I had to live in a tent for the last year and I thought I was done with that shit. The unit loaded up and convoyed out to the middle of nowhere, and I flew out in an H-13 owned by the 2nd A.D. It didn't take me long to realize they have no concept of how to utilize a helicopter. I start making up my own plans, and this way I got to fly as much as I wanted, and also had to return to the army base for maintenance and fuel.

This was my chance to get away from this bunch on a regular basis. I had slept one night in the tent and damn near died. Seems no one thought that they might need a heater, for a tent out in the desert in the middle of the winter. Plus, I'm back eating those damn C-rations again. The lieutenants are all sitting around spooning those cold rations out of the cans and thinking this was as good as it gets. Not enough exposure to a warrant officer with a tour in V.N. It took me about five minutes to sort through the discarded cans and make myself a field stove. Then it was a trip to the H-13 to fill the can with gas and back to the tent. I selected a couple of meals that I liked and mixed them together. I took some cheese from the packet with the crackers and threw that in. Find the salt, pepper and creamer from the little condiments pack, and added that for taste. Heat and stir and I had a meal fit for a king while they all sit and stare at me. It took those Lts. about ten seconds to know that I had tricks they had never seen, and they wanted to learn all about them.

These Jr. officers also needed to learn about helicopters, and the role they play as a scout for armor. I set up training flights to take them up one at a time for a look see, and orientation. But before we go I extract a little quid pro quo. They want to fly in my bird. Fine. I get to drive their tanks. Talk about cool. I sat up front in the drivers spot and had this set of controls with a steering yoke, brakes and gas and I can run over anything that I want to. It is up and down dry washes and through mesquite trees, churning up dirt and dust. I had always wanted to drive something that big and now was my chance. The trade off was flying these Lt's around at tree top lever, scaring them and making a couple of them puke. That was even better.

Somehow I always managed to need to go to the airfield for gas or maintenance on the -13. No one had a clue about how much gas I could carry or how often the crew chief needed to perform some repairs. I simply told the commander I had to head back to the airfield, and off I go. After the first night in the tent, I spent the rest of the week home in my own bed. I just had to get up early and fly back out to the field training site each morning. A couple of days of this, the tankers were so busy running around playing army, that they didn't seem to need my services. So I just kind of disappeared back to the main airfield.

# I CAN'T SPEL ENSTRUKTOR. NOW I ARE ONE

The 2nd A.D. flight detachment started making calls to the Cav. to get me released to them for flying. They had a bunch of H-13s and a couple of Hueys, but no one to cross train the pilots to the -13. The next thing I knew I'd been transferred and had orders, assigning me to temporary duty at Ft. Wolters, TX., to learn to become an instructor pilot. The army requires formal classes before you are put on orders as an instructor. Two of my new friends are also sent along to become instructors so off we go for a one week class. One was Loren McAnnaly and I can't remember the other pilot. I do remember we drove up to Wolters in Mac's GTO convertible. At some point the 8-track player ate the one good tape, so we decided to do a field expedient fix. We pulled all of the tape out of the box and had it strung all over the inside of the car. We took turns trying to get it re-wound. Somewhere along Hwy 281 the tape joined the sage brush. *Goodbye Credence.*

On the very first day of flying, I was up with my instructor and listening to the air to air chatter on the radio. There was a mayday call coming over the radio, and an instructor and student reported they have lost the main rotors off their helicopter and were going down. We listened to them scream all the way to the ground. When I got back that day, I found out the instructor who was killed was an old class mate of mine, Peter Hooper, who had survived combat in Vietnam only to die in Texas. Hoop had been a source of real humor when we were together in flight school. He had this knack of being able to sleep with his eyes open. We would be in some class and he would doze off, and start snoring. The instructor would hear it and start looking around trying to find whoever was daring to sleep during his lecture. Hoop would just sit there looking like everyone else, but was catching up on some needed rest.

We finished up our course of instruction and returned to Ft. Hood. I was told that I now was on orders, to become the 6th Army Standardization Instructor Pilot (S.I.P)for the H-13. The 6th Army was basically the entire western U.S. and I was now the instructor of the instructors, plus I would have to test them each year and give a check ride to the instructors to make sure they knew what they were doing. I got to spend just about every day flying the -13 around the area, and training everyone how to fly it. When I'm not doing that I'm working with the other two instructors making sure they stay proficient, and giving them check rides. I have to test their proficiency and sign them off so they can stay instructors. *"O.K. Let's take off and climb to 500 feet. Now point the nose toward Lake Belton. See if you can find a tavern with a large empty parking lot. If you do, and you buy, I'm pretty sure you pass your check ride."*

Being an army S.I.P. had also now led to one of the best jobs I ever had. The Commanding General of the 2nd A.D. General Shea, had gone to flight school, but didn't finish. During his training he was a colonel, but got selected to get his first star. But with that, he had to leave flight training and take over a unit in Korea. Now he was back in the U.S and the one thing he really wants is to finish his flight training. So guess who gets to fly him around Ft. Hood and re-teach him all he needs, to be awarded his wings? Seems that as an S.I.P, I can award wings to those that qualify, and pass the training syllabus.

Once or twice a week the general's aide would call and inform me that the "Man" wanted to do some flight training, and would meet me at the airfield. He always arrived carrying a Snoopy lunch box that his wife had fixed for him. In it were a couple of p.b and jelly sandwiches, cookies and a thermos of coffee. I always welcomed the general and informed him about what we would be doing, and that as the instructor I was in charge of the helicopter and the training. He would look at me and remind me that I might be in charge in the air, but as soon as we touched back down at the airfield, "I'll be back in charge, so don't piss me off." He had a great sense of humor and it was a really easy relationship. We had a great time.

We would do some maneuvers around the airfield then head out to cover some cross country and take off and landings from confined areas. He loved to visit people in his unit and drop in on them without any notification. It was always a great pleasure to watch the face of some tank commander who just had the general drop in from out of nowhere, and ask what he was up to. I also remember a time when he spotted a jeep driving around the desert and decided to stop it and talk to whoever was driving. We got in front of the jeep and got it stopped and the general hopped out. In the jeep was a private, who now found himself talking to "God", but the general was truly a gentleman and had the private at ease in a moment or two. The next thing he did was have me shut down the helicopter and bring the lunch box. So the three of us sat out there in the desert and shared the sandwiches while General Shea asked this kid a million questions about his life in the 2nd A.D. He always wanted to know if they had problems and what he could do to help. Did his bosses treat him o.k.? Did he like his job? Sometimes we would spend a half hour with whoever we dropped in on, and it was always great fun for me because all these colonels, majors, captains, and lieutenants were also watching and getting to know who was the general's pilot.

This had the additional benefit of me always being treated to drinks at the officers club. I would walk in and before too long some officer would send over a drink, and then follow that up with a little visit. They always wanted to be sure I remembered their names, and to give General Shea their best regards. A lowly warrant officer 2 and it was as if they forgot who outranked who. I held the keys to the throne and the ear of the king. I loved it.

# GIT ALONG LITTLE DOGIE

Before becoming an aviator, I always wanted to be a cowboy. Now I got my chance. One of the other little jobs I performed was, the round up of cattle on the firing range. Most of Ft. Hood was open range and the local ranches would let their cattle roam around the large training areas. Ft. Hood had missile units and they would schedule a launch from the main post into the training area. They wanted to see if they could hit what they were aiming at, but not kill someone's cows. I would get the call and conduct a one man, one helicopter, round up.

I would head out to the range area and start herding the cows back toward the main base. This required being very low and slow, and without scaring the herds, head them in the right direction. Sometimes I would run across a bull who was not about to yield to my instructions, and he would have to be nudged along. The bull would stand there with his head up glaring at me and not moving, so I would get behind him and inch up with the helicopter skids. As soon as I began poking him in the ass with the -13 he would get the idea and move to where I wanted him. It was like a challenge. He would look back over his shoulder as if to say, *"Land and come over here, and we'll see who nudges who in the ass."*

He had to show the girl cows he wasn't afraid of me until I threatened his nether region and then he'd move. This was great fun and I got to do it about once a month. I think some of the cows remembered me, because I would show up and they would just turn and head for the gate. Someone should have bought me spurs and a cowboy hat.

It was during my cowboy era that I also thought it would be great idea to own a motorcycle. My first instinct was not to buy one, but get the army to provide one for me. I went down to the maintenance office and went through the TOE for the 2nd A.D. flight detachment. The Table of Organization and Equipment listed everything that should be assigned to the unit from aircraft to trucks and desks. Lo and behold there it was, a Harley Davidson with side car, to be used by the unit for parts runs, or to transport messages. Now the Commander, Jimmy Parker, had to approve this requisition so I had to catch him in a good mood, and convince him this was one piece of equipment he could not do without. I don't know who the original author is but Parker loved to refer to this one saying whenever he was dealing with us warrant officers, especially the ones who had been to Nam. He said, "Commanding Warrant Officers is like trying to herd cats." I don't know what that has to do with me having an assigned Harley, but it took Jimmy P. about two seconds to tell me, "No, but hell no!"

Jimmy P was probably the best Commander I ever had and he was truly a nice man. I remember he had a poster of Richard Nixon on the back of his door in his office. The one with the saying, "Would you buy a used car from this man?" General Shea showed up one day and went into Jimmy's office for a briefing. When he closed the door he spotted the poster, and I think Jimmy had some explaining to do. Nixon was the elected Commander in Chief and as such was to be afforded all honor and respect. Anyway the boss wouldn't let me have a motorcycle on the Army's nickel, so off I went to the local motorcycle shop in Killeen. They mainly sold just Hondas and I found a nice little 350 Scrambler. I had to pay $200 for this thing which was a lot of money back then, but now I had independent transportation. Heleen needed to have the car, and I couldn't always catch a ride to and from work. I loved the bike. It was fast and loud and could be ridden on or off road. Warrant officer pilots, and mainly the ones who had already survived Vietnam, were all a little crazy. The parking lots were full of fast cars and motorcycles and there was nothing that wasn't tried for a little excitement. I remember one night being invited to a party at one of the pilot's homes. Heleen drove the car and I rode the motorcycle. We needed the car to haul our daughter Michelle, who always attended the parties. When we arrived Heleen parked in front and I just kept going up the front walk, and parked in the living room.

A friend of mine, Asa, also thought a motorcycle was a great idea so he went and bought one. Then George Van Riper got one. We use to spend our down time, hill climbing and racing around the airfield. One of the joys in life was screwing with your pals and fellow pilots. One of the other guys bought a bike, and rode it into work. He parked it, and then left on a mission in the Huey. Off we raced to the store and before he could get back we had a set of training wheels bolted to the rear of his new bike. He sure loved us for thinking of his safety.

# CAST OF CHARACTERS

Heleen and I ran with two different groups of pilots. We had all the warrant officers who were attached to the 2nd A.D. and almost every one of them had done a tour in Vietnam. The second group were the 1st and 2nd lieutenants who had gone through flight school, and were awaiting assignment to V.N. The first group included Loren McAnnaly, Bob Lake, Alvie Cook, Phil McMillen, Dan Zube, Merwin Beard, John Toesnsing, Bill Raney, Mike Harrington and Jim Fowler, and maybe three or four others plus Jimmy Parker, our Commander, and Chico Fernandez his Executive Officer. Chico used to get screwed with continually, but was a good sport. One time he had to go to the Division H.Q for a meeting so some of the guys went out and bought those multi colored stick on flowers. This was the Age of Aquarius and flower power, so it was only fitting that Chico's old Plymouth be decked out. Chico didn't bat an eye or remove the flowers. He simply drove all over Ft. Hood looking like and escapee from hippy heaven.

In the second group were George Van Riper and George Snyder, Gary Griffith, Jumping Joe Riley and a guy named Reed. Reed had this Jaguar XKE that he had purchased with money he had won playing golf. He was on the pro or semi-pro circuit, before getting invited to play army. He and I would roar around the back roads of Texas to see who could take the corners at the fastest speed. That car would just squat lower and lower as you went faster, and it felt like it was stuck to the pavement. It was great fun to drive. It was like flying low level in a helicopter through the grass and trees. Reed told the funniest story I had ever heard, about the Alabama Highway Patrol. When Reed was at Ft. Rucker he was out cruising one day and went through a radar trap a little fast. The cops pulled him over and told him they were going to write him a ticket for 900 miles an hour in a 55 m.p.h zone. Reed told them that their radar was incorrect and that he was in possession of a Jaguar, with a highly calibrated speedometer from Britain. He said he could prove they were wrong. He told them he would go down the road and turn around, and then drive past their radar doing 55 m.p.h He would then stop so they could see what the radar read. Reed said, "I went down about a mile and turned around. When I went past the cops doing 140 m.p.h, all they could do is stare with their mouths open. It was the last time I saw either of them."

 Riley was a new warrant officer and would soon wed wife number three. Van Riper always joked that he waited until age 26 to get wedded, and Joe went through three marriages before he was 21. Riley would soon make up a pre-printed Dear John letter that he would hand out to wives or potential wives. They just had to date and sign it. Riley was the poster child of what not to do. I taught him how to fly extremely low level with the H-13 and he went right out and hit a tree top, tearing the landing light off the bottom. Or the night he had to spend in the Copperas Cove jail for being a drunk in a car. He wasn't driving, but he was the only one with money, so the cops kept him. He finally had to call Chico to come and bail him out. Joe was also the drinking champ at the O'club but paid for it. He would get drunk and leave for the bathroom. His beer would get filled with hot sauce which he thought was just a red beer. He'd drink it down and not even notice until later when it hit his intestinal tract, and he began farting fire balls.

We also had this flight surgeon named Mike Mehegan who could never seem to get his uniform on right or with the proper insignia. The hat or shoes may or may not match or he could be wearing flip flops. One collar point of his shirt said lieutenant and the other may have a captain's bar on it. He also kept a witch doctor's mask and rattle in his office just in case he couldn't cure you using what he learned in medical school. He always inspired confidence in the medical profession

Also in this group was a new guy named Asa Crenshaw. It took us about five seconds after we met to realize we were kindred spirits. Asa and I became best friends and stayed that way for over 39 years. Only his death separated us in 2007.

Pilots who had done the tour in Nam always looked down their noses at the pilots who were cherries. We sort of lorded it over them that we had seen the Devil, and they hadn't. Of course they were jealous and they spent a lot of time calling their branch to get on orders to V.N. We were separate, but we also were brothers due to flying. The one area where we were really joined, was our love of partying.

Every single Friday the call would go out by Jimmy P, that there was a mandatory formation at the Officers Club. We would arrive and take over a large section of the club. It took us about one pitcher of beer to start challenging all the non pilots, to drinking contests. The tables were arranged so that different branches would sit together. The artillery might be at one table with the engineers or tankers at another. We challenged all and beat all. And of course we were humble winners. Whoever lost to us could be assured to find a gift for them waiting the next week when they arrived. I remember buying a sand pail and shovel and painting the engineer crest of it. We gave it to the engineers the next week, and then made them drink beer out of it. Jumping Joe always got the call for the challenge and he never lost.

As the evening progressed worried looks would start to show on some of the faces, because they knew they were going to catch hell from their wives when they got home. So the only solution was for Jimmy P to start writing notes of excuse for those needing them, and of course one of us always had to write a note for Jimmy. There were several nights when Jimmy had to spend the night on someone's couch. As the merriment continued someone would jump up and yell; "Party at Mikey's or Asa's", or some other unlucky souls. Everyone would go to pick up their bride or girlfriend and continue the party. This was an every, single Friday night event.

It was at one of these nightly get together at Bill Rancy's place when we got a call from Jimmy P, who for once had gone home to Austin. He said there was a storm coming with really high winds and we needed to get all the aircraft into the hanger. None of us was sober but that didn't stop us from obeying the boss man. We headed out to the airfield and put ground handling wheels on the helicopters, so we could tow or shove them into the hanger. There was one H-13 parked on the grass and we couldn't get the wheels installed. So our only choice was for Snyder and Van Riper to start it up and fly it to the parking area. I think the uniform for all involved, was flip flops, shorts and no helmets. If they had rolled that one up in a ball, while drunk, they would have been cell mates at Leavenworth.

Our little trailer was the unofficial headquarters for all the bachelors in the group. If it was a holiday like Christmas, they would get invited over to put a present under the tree and get one in return, plus a nice holiday meal with our family of three. Heleen had learned to make Tacos from some friends when we were stationed at Ft. Wolters during flight school. This was her specialty and everyone loved them. Sometimes we would host a dinner for the guys that were single, and invite them for tacos. Heleen would end up making over a dozen tacos per guy. I think she made more tacos than a Mexican restaurant. I don't know how we could eat so many then, and still stay skinny.

# IN A GADDA DA VIDA

That song was our anthem for some damn reason. On every turn table, at every party, on and on it went. Those 17 minutes of drum solo and a little singing was played over and over at ear splitting volume. I think everyone owned the album and probably wore it out, at least on the one side. I always think about these parties and wonder why the neighbors didn't complain or call the cops. Oh. Yeah! Usually the neighbors were at the party. And of course we never had anything but the best to drink. Annie Green Springs, Boones' Farm, Ripple and cases of imported beer from Milwaukee. Most of the parties ended up in Lake's and McAnnaly's apartment due to the simple fact that they were single, and had no one to bitch at them. Plus, they didn't care what happened to the floors, walls, appliances and ceiling. Their apartment complex also came with a pool, where someone would always end up before the night was over. They also had a couch which Jimmy P claimed, "Fit like a glove."

The other theme song that all V.N. pilots just had to hear was, "We Gotta Get Out Of This Place." If you were anywhere in Vietnam where there might be a show or music, that was the last song played of the night. There would be a Philippine or Korean band beating the shit out of American songs, and they knew the words. Everyone who could still stand up did, and at the top of our lungs we would sing along with the chorus, "We gotta get out of this place. If it's the last thing we ever do." For some reason it just seemed like the song was appropriate.

When I went back to Nam in 69' it was still being sung. The parties were a lot of fun and we did them often. I think the guys just needed stress reduction after a week of flying and of course the nightmares and bad dreams. I don't know who suffered from Post Traumatic Stress Disorder, because a guy just didn't talk to anyone else about that. The only ones who knew, were the wives who lived with it.

I think the other pilots who hadn't been to Nam, partied like us to be part of the group, or maybe they were just in training for when they arrived in the jungle. I'm sitting here trying to conjure up names and faces, and the one reality is that I cannot remember a single helicopter pilot who did not drink. Just did not happen. Or if it did they were never around the groups that I hung out with. Flying helicopters was a dangerous occupation, and a pilot never knew when his last flight might take place. So the mantra was always; "Party hard."

Our other party headquarters was Asa's place. He lived out in the country a ways, and was a bachelor with a ski boat. Enough said. Every chance we got we were on Lake Belton water skiing and drinking beer. Up and down that lake we went, raising hell and living large. Usually there would be at least a dozen involved at any time. The guys would be getting a little hammered and the wives were taking care of the kids and feeding us.

Every Friday at the O' club was followed by a gathering of eagles at someone's house or apartment. Then came Saturday night with another party at one of the homes, and then Sundays on the lake. No wonder some guys wanted to return to Vietnam, just so they could get some rest. House parties were dangerous. Pilots are free thinkers and risk takers, and not beyond a little tomfoolery. I have been accused of several incidents, but as far as I know there is no photographic proof. Also due to age I'm sure memories are a little blurry. One time I thought that the absolutely best thing I could do upon arriving at a house, was to have someone open the front door, so I could bring my motorcycle into the living room. I guess in hindsight I could have walked it in, but it was already running and I hated to push it. The burn out also endeared me to my hosts.

Bobby Lake found his niche by becoming a bathroom attendant. He would get a little drunk and go to the bathroom and remove the roll of toilet paper. He would then stand against the wall at attention with his fingers inserted in the roll, and await the ladies. After they were seated he would start singing that he was a, "Musical toilet paper dispenser" and to please take what you needed. Some of the women just didn't understand, but the rest of us thought it was hilarious.

Alvie and I were so a taken with this idea, that we decided to improve on it and the master plan was hatched. The two of us would creep into the bathroom and hide in the bath tub behind the shower curtain. I do believe that Van Riper also was in attendance, because he was so easily led astray. When the women came in to use the facility, we planned to burst into song and serenade them while they peed.

We were at our post for maybe 20 seconds, giggling and trying to be quiet when the shower curtain was ripped back and our wives grabbed us by the ears and pulled us out. Women are narrow minded and don't recognize true talent when they see it.

# TEX MEX AND MEDEVACS

The 2nd A.D. set up medevac flights to Ft. Sam Houston. I was told once that this was the first organized state side medical flights, and we were the test site. Whenever a soldier or one of their family members needed emergency care, we would pick them up and fly them down to Ft. Sam. Ft. Sam Houston was the primary Army Hospital in San Antonio, TX and provided care for burns, amputations, and head injuries. A lot of soldiers from Vietnam were sent there for skin grafts, prosthetics and care. A Huey was placed on standby every day, and the duty rotated among the pilots of the 2nd A.D. When you pulled duty you went about your normal day at the flight operations but you were restricted to the immediate area. You had to be able to get airborne as quickly as possible. In the late afternoon the crew would move the helicopter down to the air field fire station, and everyone would spend the night with the firemen, unless you got a call out.

These firemen were mostly "Tex Mex" and loved to cook and do strange things in their down time. Some of the things they did resulted in that activity ending up in the dinner. The food was always great, but you learned not to ask what the hell the meat was. I was never really sure if they were yanking our chains, or if they were serious about trapping and cooking, Texas wildlife. I know personally that these guys would go out with a can of gas, and find a rattlesnake pit and pour the gas in. Once the snakes were too screwed up on gas fumes to move, they would scoop them out and put them in sacks. I am not sure where the snakes went from there, but they could have been part of the chicken stew.

These idiots would also go out after dark with flashlights and gunny sacks. They would track a family of skunks and start at the rear, running and grabbing up the babies until they got to mother skunk, and then they would retreat back to the fire station. They were a fun loving bunch, and were always a source of storytelling and practical jokes. Of course they made me nervous. I was never sure where all their pet critters were, and hoped they weren't under my bed.

I did not like flying the medevac flights. It just bothered me to know whoever was lying in the back was so injured, that they might die before I could get them anywhere. A lot of the patients were head injuries and the medical staff in the back would be working on them while we flew. The ride to Ft. Sam was anywhere from one to two hours depending on the weather, but in those circumstances always seemed to take forever. There was nothing like a medic on the intercom wanting to know if you could possibly go faster.

But the standby duty was great. A few of the more enterprising pilots and crew, packed an overnight bag with all the essentials. Nice clothes; money; whiskey; latex. This was a large Army Hospital they were headed to, and it was filled with nurses. The Officer and NCO Clubs were lively places and were not to be missed. The crews became ingenious at finding safety violations and small part failures on their helicopter, that could only be fixed in the light of a new day.

/

"Ft. Hood Operations."

"Hello. This is Lt. Horny. It looks like we have to spend the night at Ft. Sam. The muffler bearings on the Huey went out. We should have it fixed by tomorrow morning."

"Hey! Lieutenant. You said the same thing the last time you flew to Ft. Sam."

"I cannot hear you Ft. Hood. Must be a bad connection caused by an alcoholic ingestion to the flight controller."

Click!

Life continued on in Texas. Heleen was pregnant again and we were expecting in March of 69'. I was looking to the future and had enrolled in college. I thought about what I wanted to do and since I only knew flying, that was the direction I was headed. I looked around for flying jobs and the one that seemed the coolest was being a pilot for the Los Angeles Police Department. They had a bunch of helicopters and I figured I would apply. I was now studying law enforcement and criminal justice in night school and sent LAPD a letter showing my interest. I was soon contacted by the Texas Rangers who had in turn been contacted by LAPD. A Ranger came out to the trailer to interview me for possible future employment in California, and shortly after the interview, LAPD sent a letter stating that they were offering me a job, providing I passed the tests. As soon as my military commitment was over I knew where I was headed.

Not long after this there was a cavalry unit on base that had been formed and was getting ready to deploy to Vietnam. This was a helicopter unit with Hueys and the new OH-6 LOH (light observation helicopter), and they needed to get all of their helicopters to Stockton, CA. for shipment to Vietnam. I figured this would give me a chance to take a look at L.A and firm up my plans. I volunteered to fly an LOH out to the coast, and several days later all 36 helicopters lined up and launched into the sky. We were led by a Lt. colonel who was the new commander of the cavalry unit. It did not take anyone long to find out what an incompetent leader he was.

Our first stop on the flight was Fort Bliss in El Paso. Before we got there he led us into the pass east of El Paso, which on a good day is a bit hairy. We had up drafts and down drafts so severe that the 36 birds were scattered everywhere from ground level up to several thousand feet. One second you could reach out and touch the ground and the next second you were climbing like an express elevator, and you couldn't do a damn thing to stop it. Once we were out of the pass, we had to land in the desert and allow flight crews to get out and clean the puke off their flight suits. Others had thrown up in their helmets or helmet bags, and the airplanes stank. I didn't lose my lunch but a whole bunch of crews did. When we finally landed at Fort Bliss the hoses came out and all the birds got washed down. The flight suits would get the same treatment later in the motel.

We spent the night and the next morning prepared to launch again. Next stop was Phoenix, AZ. We all lifted off in formation following the LTC, who immediately made a left turn and started south. If you know anything about geography you realize we are now in the sovereign air space of Mexico. The airport controllers are yelling at us and the LTC can't seem to figure out where to go, so we turned a couple of circles. We re-entered the U.S and then turned south again, only to get yelled at some more. Dumb shit finally figured out that the USA is north so off we go. The LTC racked up a whole bunch of flight violations which are not conducive to a flying career in the Army.

We hit Phoenix and spent the night. We landed at Phoenix International Airport which was about 1/10 the size that it is now. One of the guys in my group had family living nearby so he hooked us up with a party. I just knew I'm going to regret this in the morning when I had to fly at 6:00 a.m. I got up in the morning and ate a quick breakfast. We all headed for the aircraft and did our preflight inspections, and then the formation lifted off for California. We are being led by the inept and know it. I'm not sure where we were supposed to go next for our fuel stop, but it wasn't where we ended up. Edwards Air Force base was a restricted air base and still is. Here we were landing where we are not suppose to, and the tower is yelling at us, and the LTC is replying that he is correct and this is where we are supposed to be. The next thing we saw were jeep loads of military police surrounding us, with guns locked and loaded. The tower told us we had 30 seconds to get off his air base, and then they are going to shoot. It was not a pretty sight, when 36 helicopters all decided to exit stage left at the same time. Why no one ran into someone else, is anyone's guess.

We formed up and turned toward L.A to find gas. What I found was more damn concrete than I had ever seen. There were freeways going everywhere, and cars jammed bumper to bumper. As far as I could see there was nothing but houses and people. I decided right then and there, that maybe flying for LAPD just wasn't what I wanted. To top it off we fueled up and lifted off, and it took us several thousand feet to climb out of the smog. There was this thick brown crap from the ground up, and now I knew I didn't want to live there.

We arrived in Stockton that afternoon and turned over the helicopters for shipment overseas. They bused us to San Francisco, and we all got hotel rooms for the one night we would be there. We showered, shaved and shined up as best we could, and went out for dinner. Then of course someone suggested that as long as we were near North Beach we should maybe take in some of the cultural attractions. There were so many strip clubs that we could not choose, so we tried to hit them all. After a few beers it was beddy bye time as we had an early flight back to Texas.

The Lt. Colonel, our intrepid leader on the flight west, racked up more flight violations for the snafu at Edwards and was relieved of his command. Can you just imagine the havoc and chaos he would have created for those pilots once he was in Vietnam? We suffered through enough dumb shits in combat, so one less was a blessing.

# PEG LEG

Pilots were continually coming and going. Someone new would arrive from flight school, or return from Vietnam. When I graduated from helicopter training they couldn't wait to put my ass on the big bird, and send me off to get shot at. Now the emphasis was on forming new units in the states, and sending the pilots and their helicopters together. All of that nice additional training instead of OJT (on the job training) in the Nam.

One day, Asa got his orders sending him off to war. So of course we had to have a party or parties. Seems you can never have too many. The day of the big event was being held out at Asa's place in the country, but I was going to be late. Heleen had decided to head for Washington to visit family, so I had to drive her to Dallas to catch a plane. If I hurried though I would be able to catch the latter part of the festivities. After a hectic round trip I was back at Asa's but there was no one there. I called around and found out Asa was in the Hospital, and was in critical condition from an accident. He had a beer or two and thought that he could ride his motorcycle. He piled on with his current girlfriend, and off they went for a little spin. He came around a corner on the two lane, and there stood some kids in the middle of the road. His only choices were run into them or go off the highway.

He took the latter and hit a tree which ripped his knee off. The girl friend did not have a scratch on her. By the time I got to the hospital they had already amputated Asa's leg, and he was in the ICU recovering from surgery. It did not take the girl friend long to figure out, she had not signed on for a one legged helicopter pilot. She was never to be seen again after one visit to the hospital.

Myself and several of the pilots hung out on a daily basis until Asa started his recovery period, then it was decided what he really needed was to go to the Officers Club for rehab. Asa had a nurse assigned to him named Marti, who also hung around with one of our groups, and would party with us. Whenever Marti was on duty in the ICU, myself and another pilot, usually Bob Lake, would put on our dress uniforms with all our medals and other bullshit. We always dressed to impress, and found that no one seemed to question what we were doing. Marti knew, but always turned a blind eye. We would march in like we owned the place, and get Marti to release Asa to us for special rehab. We of course would take him directly to the O' Club and get him knee walking drunk. Or as shit faced as you could get with just one knee. When we brought him back to the hospital Marti would read us the riot act, forgive us, and give us a kiss goodbye. A few days later we would do it all over again.

One night we were sitting at the bar in the Officers Club and Asa is full of himself and feeling no pain when a young 2nd Lt. came in and sat on the stool next to him. A short time went by when all of sudden I hear a wham, and the Lt. is lying on the floor unconscious. I asked Asa what the hell did he do to this guy and he replied, "I just asked him if he had ever seen a shark? When he said no, I pulled up my empty pant leg and showed him mine." When they cut off Asa's leg they sewed the gaping wound shut with wire, and it looked just like a big mouth. Where the leg bones had been it looked like two eyes above the mouth, so it kind of made a goofy looking shark face.

A few weeks later, Asa had been fitted with a wooden leg and was learning to use it, so we figured the best place to practice was the O' Club. If he could drink and walk, then he was well on his way to recovery. We were again sitting at the bar when some Army Ranger came in and sat next to Asa. Asa sat there for a while then turned to the ranger and asked him, "Do you think you're tough?" The guy mumbled something and Asa replied, "I'll show you tough." With that he pulled out his pocket knife, opened it up, and then stuck it in his wooden leg. This poor ranger had no idea that Asa had a prosthesis and damn hear lost his lunch as Asa wiggled the knife around and then pulled it back out of his leg.

During the next couple of months, Asa and Marti fell in love and decided to get married. I was to be best man and my daughter Michelle was going to be the flower girl. Heleen was as big as a house and getting ready to give birth to daughter number two, so she was assigned to just sprawl in one of the pews. Marti had no family living anywhere nearby, so Jimmy Parker got the honor of giving Marti away. Asa and Marti set up house and would often come over and steal Michelle and keep her for one or two days. Heleen would have to call them and threaten them if they didn't return her. I think the two of them decided to get married just so they could have kids of their own to spoil.

The wedding date arrived and Asa and I were standing in the back of the chapel. He had on a suit and his new leg and was staying upright by using a pair of crutches. The ceremony got started and now it was our turn to take the walk down the aisle. Asa turned to me and said, "If I am getting married, I am damned if I will do it on crutches." I asked what he wanted me to do and he said, "Just stay behind me in case I fall." With that the crutches got tossed on a chair and with me on his elbow away we went. It was a long damn walk and by the time we got to the front of the church he was sweating big time, and I was crying like a baby. After the ceremony we got out the Jack Daniels to ease the pain, and the rest of the night was a bit of a blur.

Finally Monica arrived and Michelle now had a baby sister. She immediately took charge of Monica and of course everything else. She took this job so seriously that one time when Asa and Marti were over; Asa took his leg off to rest the sore spots and then couldn't find it later, when it was time to go home. Michelle was asked if she had seen the leg, and she announced that she had put the leg to bed. Sure enough there it was all tucked in for the night in the spare bedroom.

The Army was threatening to retire Asa based on his disability. As fellow pilots we could not have that happen, so we use to sneak Asa out to the flight line and into a Huey. We then let him fly the helicopter around and get used to handling it again. The big hurtle we had to overcome, was Asa not being able to hover. A helicopter takes two hands and two legs at all times especially when near the ground. Asa just couldn't get that wooden leg to push the pedal in. Asa was grounded, but not out of the Army. They found jobs he could do and kept him on for a few years longer, then medically retired him. He and Marti eventually packed up their two children and moved to Tucson, AZ., where Marti continued her nursing career and Asa began a new one with the U.S Forest Service.

This was an idyllic time. We had our own little home and two children to spoil. A ton of friends who were more like family, and ideal flying conditions around Texas. Then the phone call was made.

# VIETNAM REDUX

I guess I just couldn't leave well enough alone, so I decide to call my Warrant Officer Aviation Branch, and see what was coming up for me. This idea didn't just come out of the blue. Lots of veterans had the itch to go back. I don't think it was patriotism as much as a need to experience the adrenaline rush again. There was also a lot of guilt. Other pilots were fighting and dying, and even though you might not tell anyone about your feelings, there was a strong calling to do your part. The job just wasn't done. Plus, that trouble maker Joe Riley was getting ready to go to Nam, and kept after everyone to join him.

I called the Pentagon, and they told me they were just getting ready to send me orders to return to Vietnam. It seems that they had a real need for crazy assholes that could and would, fly low level recon missions for the scouts. Branch said that they already had me on orders to attend the OH-6 transition course. I said; "No, but hell no. I ain't going. I'll go to Canada." I argued with them for a while then they finally said, how about Chinook training instead? Now the Chinook is a nice big tandem rotor beast with twin engines. It's expensive and they don't like to risk having them shot down. So I said, "OK. I'll do Hooks, but when I get orders to a unit, I ain't going back to the god damn 1st Cav."

Orders arrived sending me to Ft. Rucker for Chinook transition and then on to the replacement depot (Repo Depot) in Vietnam for assignment. My next chores were to get Heleen and the girl's home to Washington and then pack up the trailer and have it shipped. They will need a place to live while I'm gone again. I got everyone off on the plane, and then the movers picked up the trailer. I loaded the car and drove to Alabama to begin Hook training.

The Ch-47 Chinook is a great bird. It had twin engines and tandem rotors. It also had five different transmissions to make the whole mess work. Everything was run off of hydraulics, and there were approximately 5 miles of lines inside to carry all the fluid. Of course this just means there are more things that can go wrong. I learned all the basic flight characteristics of the Hook and I spend a lot of time doing internal and external loads. The Chinook is also designed to carry a large amount of troops at one time. The Huey can carry 8 fully loaded troops, and a Hook can carry about 30. The Huey can get into smaller areas, but it requires more helicopters and more trips. It's also smaller and makes for less of a target. I can hear all of those slick drivers rolling over in their graves right now. The Hook can carry more troops and equipment, but is a much larger and more expensive target. It also requires a parking lot to land in. You can load a couple of jeeps inside a Hook and hang another one below it on straps. It is a real work horse.

I learned how to make running take offs and running landings. The Chinook had wheels that are steerable and brakes to bring it to a stop. Later back in Vietnam I loved to show off when coming into an airfield with a nice runway. I would flare the -47 and kiss the tarmac with the rear wheels, and then keep the nose pointed at the sky and taxi down the ramp. With a delicate touch I would stop and then gently lower the front wheels to the ground. This always impressed the other helicopter pilots, but in reality it was not that tough to do. Made me feel like an airplane driver.

I also did cross country flights and a couple of overnighters. The favorite stopping place was Ft. McClelland, AL. It was about a two hour flight and was up in the pine forests. It was also the WAC (Women's Army Corp) training center at that time, and some of the pilots figured they might get lucky. The school cadre talked about the pilots, who loaded a sports car in the back and took it with them on cross country trips, so they could cruise around town wherever they were. They finally got caught and had their pee pees whacked. I was duly warned. In Viet Nam I ended up doing exactly that. Only it was O.D colored jeeps that got loaded in the back of the Hook. Whenever I went to town, I made sure I had transportation for the crew.

One day the instructor told me to be extra careful on my preflight and make sure that everything was sealed up tight. We then proceed out to a local lake, and made water landings and take offs. The CH-47 floats or at least it is designed to float. I am guessing if you had too many holes in the bottom from enemy fire that this could present a problem. Hole or no holes it sure as hell floated better than an H-13.

Eight weeks of school and I graduated and then drove cross country as fast as I could. I wanted to spend time with my family before I flew across the big pond to Vietnam. You just had no idea how fast time can fly by when you are home on 30 day leave, awaiting shipment to a war zone. Family and friends all want to see you, and of course there are parties so everyone can say goodbye again. I try and look back and recount what I did before I headed to Vietnam again, but it is all just a blur. It was the same with the days before I shipped to Nam the first tour. There are just no memories there.

I flew into Ben Hoa which is the largest base in Vietnam. This is the headquarters where the war was being directed. I got assigned to a small room and every day it was the same ordeal. Eat breakfast. Eat lunch. Sit around all day waiting for the list of orders to get posted in the afternoon. If not on orders that day, then go eat dinner. Every night I went to the local Officers Club and drank with all the other pilots waiting on orders. I would repeat this as many times as necessary. On the third day, I was standing in line waiting to read the list of names and unit assignments. I moved to the front and scanned the sheet. There it was. Lazares, Michael D. WO-2, 228th ASHB, 1st CAV. "Oh no!" There has to be a mistake. I am not doing that again.

I ran for a phone, and called the assignment group that did this to me. I spent about an hour on the phone pleading with them, and telling them I was promised anything but the Cav. I told this faceless person: "I will go AWOL. I'll skip the country and go to Thailand or Canada or Australia. I will slit my wrists." I had spent that first tour sleeping in a tent, on the ground and in the helicopters. I ate crappy food, and drank warm beer, if and when I could get it. I am not doing it again. Finally I heard what I want to hear. I was told that the orders will be cancelled and I will have a new set tomorrow. I wiped the tears of joy off of the phone, and headed for the O' Club to celebrate.

The following morning I got a message to report to the Commander of the Repo Depot. When I showed up I had to explain why I caused all of the turmoil, but a smile came over the colonel's face, and he told me that he does not blame me a bit. I was then handed orders sending me to the 196th ASHC, Lane Army Airfield. This is back in the area of Qui Nhon, where I had spent most of the first tour, and I'm a happy camper.

I loaded up my bags and reported to the air field for transportation north. As I was waiting I found this brand new 2nd Lt. who had just finished flight school and was assigned to the same airfield at Lane, but with a Huey lift company. Now I am not saying Lee was a cherry, but he was one nervous dude. He had no clue what to expect or how to go about getting where he needed to go. So I told him that he was now in my capable hands and I'd show him the way. The first thing I did was get our flight changed to an airfield about a third of the way to where we had to be. I had friends from Ft. Hood flying Chinooks there, and figured it would be a great time to visit.

Alvie Cook got in-country a month or so before me and is flying Hooks with Loren McAnally at the 180th ASHC. Lt Lee starts to babble that he has to get to his unit or he'll be in trouble, and I promise that this will just be a short stop over to say hi.

# AWOL

We arrived at the 180th and I called the unit and found out Alvie was out flying, but someone would be over to pick us up, and can we spend the night? "Hell Yes." McAnnally showed up and we headed over to the unit, were shown a bunk, and then pointed toward the O' Club. I never met a Chinook unit that didn't have their own bar. When you are flying that big beast all over hauling supplies to the units, it seems that stuff just kind of falls off. Lumber and air conditioners, windows, and doors. Bar glasses and stools. There were always a couple of guys who knew how to build stuff, and before you knew it, SHAZAM! A cocktail lounge appeared. It was just like magic.

We threw our stuff on the beds and headed for the club to cut the trail dust. Here we are introduced to a quaint tradition of these particular aviators. First guy in the club drinks a couple of beers and then stands on a chair behind a giant floor fan, with his pants around his ankles. The fan was pointed at the front door, and the standee is positioned to baptize whoever arrives next. I am sure you have heard the term, "Pissing in the wind", well this adds a whole new dimension. Pretty soon the door flew open, and the pisser tries to anoint his brethren. They duck and weave and he pretty much just sprays the floor and wall. They tackled him and tried to kill him, and then threw him out the front door in the dirt. So began another night of partying.

Lee and I had to get up the next morning and call our units to tell them we were on our way. But we were delayed due to weather, or no airplanes to ride on, or we were under attack, or we can't find our ass this morning. I am in no hurry, and Lee can't wait, but he's starting to see my reasoning. When you get to Vietnam you are committed to a tour of 365 days. Every day counts no matter what you are doing. Be it flying, or on R & R, or lying around some club getting drunk. Every day is a day off that sentence. So now with time in Bien Hoa and our tour of the country side, we have already shaved about a week off our tour.

We spent three days with Alvie and Mac then needed to move on. Our units were starting to yell at us to get our asses in gear. We needed a lift so we headed to the local Air Force base to see what was available and going our way. We next found ourselves in Nha Trang at the Special Forces headquarters. "Lee. This will be just a short stop and then we'll go to our units. I promise." We got us a room for the night in the Bachelor Officers Quarters and then headed for the Officers Club. That night they had a show going on and also a going away party for the unit Chaplin. They had about eight tables butted together, forming a giant U shape. At the head of the table was the Chaplin, who had either gotten drunk on his own or with the help of the Green Beanies. Pretty soon a Philippine stripper showed up and started dancing up and down on the tables. When she got to the Chaplin, she was buck naked and ended up in his lap. I didn't know who this Chaplin was or what his history involved, but he did not seem all that unfamiliar with his situation. I'm sure God forgave him. He was just a victim of the, "Beanie Wearing Snake Eaters."

The next day I found us a ride to another army base, where it just so happened that more friends were also flying Chinooks. What an opportunity to renew friendships, so off we went. I promised Lee we would just make a quick stop over, and then head for our units at Lane AAF. Well one thing led to another and here we were with some more pilots to hang out with, and maybe have a little drink or two. This was a strange collection of pilots and the major who commanded them was the strangest of them all. Lee got assigned to a bunk and the major said I could bunk in his room, which was quite large and had an extra bed. I guess I should have listened to the guys, when they said that their C.O was just a little unhinged.

His latest escapade had taken place a couple of days before we got there, and some parts of that incident were still going on. The major thought the guys needed some in house R & R so he got drunk, got into a 2 ½ ton truck and drove down town. He then proceeded to load the back with hookers and drove them back to the unit. But first he had to get through the check point at the gate. He could stop and explain why an intoxicated major was driving a truck load of hookers for his pilots, or he could simply just run the gate and hope for the best. He ended up with the truck and bar girls at the unit club, locked inside, while the M.Ps yelled at him to come out. They finally gave up and left when someone who was sober, convinced them it was all harmless fun.

Most of the girls found their way home the next day, but it was rumored that a couple were still hiding out in some of the pilot's rooms, and may have even been going on sightseeing rides in the helicopters. They were probably sitting in some warrant officer's lap helping him steer. *"Oh! Mr. Pilot. What a big cyclic you have. I think I love you long time. No bullshit. You buy me Honda?"*

We all sat that first night in the club and drank and lied, and then it was time for bed. I headed over to the major's hooch and got undressed and into bed. All of a sudden there was a lot of commotion going on outside, followed by a pack of dogs barking. The door flew open and in came the C.O, with about 15 dogs' right behind him. He flopped down on his bed and the dogs started finding places to sprawl. Half a dozen crawled onto his bed and a couple decided to sleep with me. The rest just flop wherever. What a night, and I vowed to myself to find another bed tomorrow.

The next morning Lee and I called in to our units again. We gave them some more lies as to why we weren't where we are supposed to be. The warnings are becoming more direct, with threats of courts martial or beheading. My reply to the nervous Lee was, "What are they going to do? Send you to Vietnam." He's starting to whine that they'll charge him with being AWOL, and ruin his career. I told him with any luck he would probably get shot and killed while flying in Vietnam, and not have to worry about a career. My unit went so far as to tell me they were going to send a Chinook down for me and I had better be ready. I begged off and told them we were on a flight later that day. Of course I had no intention of going anywhere and we continued to party for two more days. We finally headed north to our new homes. Now I had about two weeks less time to put in on my tour of duty. Did I feel guilty? Not one little bit.

# REGGIE ROCK, COMMANDING

I arrived at the 196<sup>th</sup> ASHC just in time for cocktails. I met my new commander who I will call LTC. Rock. Not his real name but then you will see why in a little while. I said hello and he acted like I'm the answer to all his prayers. Boy! was he glad to see me, and what kept me so long, from getting to the unit. I later learned from the other pilots that Reggie is crazy and has been known to fire pilots on a whim. He may just walk up to someone who has done something wrong, or suspected of doing something wrong, and tell them to go pack and find a new home. I was a witness to this one time when we got two new pilots in. They reported to Reggie at our little O' Club and he looked them and their orders over. He then calmly told both of them he didn't want them, and for them to go find a new unit. We were always shorthanded of pilots, and here was Reggie getting rid of two guys we needed.

Reggie liked to sit in the bar every night and get shit faced. He would drink Old Crow straight and keep going, until he either did something really stupid like fire a pilot, or he would pass out. When this happened a couple of the pilots would bundle him up and deposit him in his room. I was watching Reggie one night and noticed his head starting to nod down toward the bar top, which was a slab of concrete. I got tired of waiting up for him to pass out, so I clicked off the lights. I heard a thump and turned the lights back on. Reggie was just picking his head up off the bar and looking dazed and confused. So I turned the lights off again. I waited until I heard the bonk and then turned them back on. Now he had a small knot rising on his forehead. I liked to humor myself as much as the next person. I went over to the bar and fixed myself a scotch on the rocks, drug a chair over to the light switch, and went back to flicking them on and off. I think it took a half hour for the small knot to become a big knot, and for blood to start trickling down Reggie's face. Reggie was barely conscious, so I went and found a couple of guys to help carry him to bed. They took a look at Reggie and asked what the hell I had done to the C.O. When I demonstrated my new hobby, they thought that it was a hoot and wanted to try it. So I let them. Word got around the unit later and it wasn't long until this became something of a semi-nightly occurrence. It was our only way to pay the son of a bitch back. Or so I thought.

About two months later we were sitting in the club drinking one night when we heard two loud booms. We killed the lights and hit the floor. We never got hit at Lane Army Air Field because the Koreans would not allow it, so we were a little shocked. Pretty soon one of the pilots came into the club to explain what happened. Reggie had a large room all to himself, that was shaped like an L. When you entered the room, straight ahead was his bed. You would then turn right and enter his living room/bathroom area. On this particular night Reggie had gotten drunk and was carried to his bed and tossed on. For some reason a little later he got up and wandered into his living room area, and again passed out on his floor. A person or persons unknown showed up, opened Reggie's door and rolled two hand grenades under his bunk. It was dark and for all he or they knew, Reggie was where he had been left. The grenades blew the shit out of his bed, but didn't put a scratch on Reggie. Within a day Reggie was gone and we had a new C.O.

# LYING WITH THE ZOOMIES

A month before Reggie left us, I found myself the recipient of a nice surprise. I got called in to the HQ by Reggie and told that if I wanted a little vacation, there was a quickie R & R to the Philippines open. Whoever had put in for the trip had changed his mind, and now it was up for grabs. I don't know why Reggie picked me but he did. I said, "Yes" and left the office to go pack. I started borrowing clothes from everyone, so that I would have civilian attire to wear once I got to Manila. I was talking to one of the pilots who had gone to the Philippines a couple of months earlier  and he told me that I should skip Manila, and stay at Clark AFB instead. He said, "It is just like being in America. They have movie theatres, stores, ice cream parlors, Officer Clubs,  and lots of Americans running around." I was really tired of Asia and Asians, and thought a change of scenery would be great.

I flew into Clark AFB on a C-130 which was loud and drafty, but no one was shooting at me. After I got orientated I got a very nice room at the BOQ and headed for the O' Club for some needed refreshments. As near as I could tell I was the only Army Aviator in the room. I got myself a table and was surrounded by guys telling me that they all flew jets over North Vietnam. I kept hearing, "Yeah! Let me tell you about the time I had two Migs chasing me. I zoomed into a tight turn, did a back flip while lighting my cigar, and then nailed both those suckers."Of course you did!

I quietly told them, "I'm just a helicopter pilot, but I have been shot down several times and wounded. Oh! By the way. I once pulled an F-4 pilot out of the South China Sea, when he got shot down by a rice farmer with an old AK-47." There is an old saying, "The first liar doesn't stand a chance." I have one upped them, and now become a celebrity. Drinks started coming my way, and I figured this trip wouldn't be so bad after all. The next few days I just hung around reading, watching TV, and taking in a couple of movies. I didn't have much desire to head to Angel City, which was outside the main gate. There was nothing there to draw my interest. I had all the cheap souvenirs I needed back at the 196th, but I did go down town one day just to look around.

I was walking around Angel City just soaking up the local flavor, when I decided to find a bar and have a cold beer. I turned a corner, spotted a bar and headed toward it when I encountered what looked like a sidewalk popcorn cart. As I neared it I thought my eyes were playing tricks on me. Inside the cart is a dead baby going around on a spit over hot coals. I couldn't believe what I was seeing and turned around to find someone to tell me it ain't so. An Airman was coming out of the bar and I told him, "Hey! They are cooking a little baby on a Barbeque." He said not to worry, that the baby is a monkey. It's just one of the local "McMonkey" franchises. He told me that another local delicacy can be found in certain restaurants. They take a live monkey and strap him into a table with a hole in the middle. The monkey just had the top of his head showing. The chef then took a real sharp machete and swung it across the table, cutting the top of the monkeys head off. Then the diners scoop out the live brains and eat them. "Yummy". That's all the local culture I can handle. I headed back to the Officers Club for a steak. I just got here it seems and I have pack for the trip back to reality. Wow! As usual the only time that doesn't fly by, is the time in Vietnam.

I reported back in to the commander and he told me that he has a surprise for me. He took me into his office and informed me that he is putting me in for a Distinguished Flying Cross. This is for the time I saved 33 Korean soldiers and my crew of 4, by not burying the helicopter in a rice paddy. This incident had occurred a couple of weeks before I went to the Philippines. All I have to do was sign this two page affidavit Reggie had already filled out. This nomination told of all the heroic deeds Reggie had accomplished as the Aircraft Commander, while engaged in aerial combat, while I just sat there and begged him to not get me killed. According to this written account, our intrepid boss not only pulled a John Wayne and single handed saved the outpost under attack, he led all the other pilots, and by example spurred them on to greatness.

Reggie gave me an Awards Nomination form, that stated a whole bunch of lies about what he did and I witnessed as his co-pilot. While I was gone on my R&R to the Philippines, the unit became involved in bringing in ammo and supplies to a Green Beret outpost that was in danger of being overrun by the NVA. The flying was real hairy and the weather was miserable, plus the NVA were doing their damn best to keep any helicopters out of the camp. I had already been told all the facts by the other pilots and knew Reggie had not even left Lane AAF. I told Reggie that not only was I not signing it, but he can shove my DFC where the sun don't shine.

I am now on Reggie's' shit list, and I found out later that he got another pilot to sign the award nomination. I wonder what he was promised. I talked to the Executive Officer about what was going on, and I was told that I was still getting the DFC from when I fell off the mountain. I was later given the medal by the new commander as an impact award.

# CLUB MED

I became the assistant Operations Officer which meant that I helped the Ops Officer plan missions, and assign the pilots to fly them. We would get a list the night before of what units needed what items. Where we would pick the stuff up at, and drop it off. We supported the Korean army a lot and they in turn provided security for our base. Every few days we would also do combat assaults into the jungles and mountains, with either American or the Korean combat troops.

The worst part about being the Ops Officer was assigning pilots to the shitty jobs. Places where they might get shot at or the flying was really hairy because of the mountains or jungle. And of course we had pilots that would screw with the system. Two of these guys were on their first tour, and had spent time in college before going to flight school. They had been exposed to the devil weed and had not broken the habit. They would be set up for a flight, but you couldn't raise them because they were locked in their room getting high. They were a couple of selfish assholes who would rather let some other pilot pull the mission, than do it themselves. Sometimes they would even come to me the night before, and ask to be given a down day so they could get wrecked. At least this way I knew they couldn't be counted on, and could shuffle the schedule.

I also picked up the task of being in charge of our little Officers Club. This was really a pretty nice building of about 800 sq. feet with a long bar made from river rock and concrete. The club sat up on the highest hill around and the back deck looked down on the Korean compound. We had a barbeque outside and some chaise lounges and assorted deck chairs. I kept the book which contained everyone's name, and when you got yourself a beer, pop or cocktail you marked it in the book. At the end of the month I would tally up what was owed and collect. This was all on the honor system and worked fine until I needed to collect. That's when I would find the non-drinker with about $50 in liquor purchases, or the jokester who marked everything on his co-pilots page. People would start bitching that they were not paying, and I would inform them that if they did not, I would ban them from the bar. That was a punishment that had some teeth to it.

After I collected I purchased more snacks, reel to reel tapes and booze and would take what was profit, and throw a party. I would catch a flight down to Qui Nhon and visit the commissary where I was able to pick up food items we never had in the mess hall. I might cook up a large ham with all the trimmings or throw a barbeque with some steaks. It sure beat the hell out of what we were eating the rest of the time.

I also paid our Vietnamese bar boy, Duke, his wages. He got free room and board. Duke was from the local village and was basically hiding out so he wouldn't get drafted by either side. The V.N. Army would come into the villages and sign up all the young men age 17 and over, and would at some point then draft them into the army. It was sort of like the U.S draft that was going on. If you had pull or you were going to school then you might be exempt from the Viet army. There was no exemption from the Viet Cong. They would come into the villages at night, and just kidnap your ass and make you a soldier. Either way wasn't pleasant, so we kept Duke hidden out on base where he was nice and safe. He had a little room fixed up next to the bar, and his job was doing whatever needed doing. He might be a janitor or carpenter or clean the bar during the day, and I put him to work behind the bar getting beers and sodas for the guys at night. I had no idea how old Duke was, but I'm pretty sure he was in his early 20s. He was there before I arrived and he was there when I left. I heard later that Duke went on one of his clandestine visits to see family in the village, and was captured up by one of the two armies. He was never seen or heard from again.

The village wasn't very safe during the day and scary at night. We had one pilot who literally locked himself in his room and refused to fly, but would go to the village every night. He had already done a tour of duty like some of us, but now he had convinced himself that if he went out flying again he would die. So at night he would sneak out and crawl through the perimeter wire, and go down to the same village Duke was from. He would then spend the night with his Viet girl friend, and then sneak back to the base in the morning. I asked Duke about this one time, and he said that the guy was left alone because the Viet Cong thought he was crazy. Maybe he was crazy like a fox. He didn't have to fly all day and he was getting laid every night.

# MAYDAY MAYDAY

**"Oh! Never mind. If I just take off my chicken plate, and then bend way over, maybe I can kiss my ass goodbye".**

A few weeks before Reggie left us I experienced an epiphany. Or maybe I just crapped my pants and thought God was speaking to me. This was the incident prior to my little time off at Clark Air Force Base.

We did a lot of combat assaults with the Koreans and most of them were pretty routine. With the Chinook you had to have a fairly large area to set that beast down. The Koreans didn't do exits using ladders and ropes, like some of the U.S troops. You would fly in and land. Down would come the ramp, and out they went with all their equipment. On big missions the ops officer or the assistant ops (me), would take a ride out with the Korean ops officer on a Huey. We would look over the area we would be putting the assault into and pick out landing zones. You might have one major assault going into a large rice paddy, or you may have multiple landings in different LZ's.

The Koreans wanted to stage an assault on the mountain peaks to the west of Lane AAF and work their way down to the valley. We had about eight different LZs picked out and I assigned my crew the toughest one. It sat on the side of the mountain, and did not have a flat spot on it. The only way we could get in and drop the troops off, was to come to a hover in midair and then back the Chinook into the mountain. Once you were close, then the crew chief would lover the ramp so it touched the side of the hill. The Koreans would have to exit the ramp and turn down the hill, to keep from getting their heads cut off by the rear rotors. This was hairy for everyone. To make matters worse, there was a tall tree right in the middle of this LZ.

I was flying and came to a nice hover in front of the drop off spot. Looking straight out I could not see anything but sky, and if I looked down through the chin bubble I could see the valley floor about 4000 feet, straight down. The crew chief was laying on the ramp and guiding me back with little tiny corrections. "Back one inch. Forward a smidge. A touch to the right. Hold it right there." I did not want to smack the mountain as that would ruin my whole day, and I did not want to get up close and personal with the tree. I tried to get close enough to drop the ramp and off load the Korean combat troops but it just wasn't working. I made about five attempts and had sweat running off me in rivulets. The crew chief was telling me, "Move it back two feet Sir. Ok. Now move it a bit to the right. Stop. Stop. Now I'll try the ramp."

I would be holding that bird as rock steady as I could and waiting for the chief to tell me what was going on. I then heard him say, "The hill is too steep. I put the ramp down and there is still no room for them to get off." The Koreans would have had to run up the ramp which was at a 30 to 40 degree up angle. Then once they were on top of the ramp they would have had to jump to the side of the mountain. Then they had to crawl away from the helicopter, so they didn't get decapitated.

Then the other pilot said, "Let me have it. I know I can do it." He grabbed the controls and started backing into the mountain and the crew chief was yelling at him to stop. BAM! He hit the tree with the aft three rotor blades. Just that quick we were out of control and falling down the side of the mountain. The helicopter was bucking and bouncing, and literally throwing us all over the cockpit. I was strapped in tight and I still couldn't stay in my seat. Both of us are on the controls and there is no way we can hang on, or make them go where we want. He was yelling on one frequency that we are going in and I was on the guard channel yelling: "Mayday. Or maybe it was Mommy."

At this point we were totally out of control and going straight into the jungle 4000 feet down, with a crew of five and thirty three Koreans. I want everyone to know about this, as maybe I will be a survivor needing to be rescued, or at least they can find some small parts to mail home to my family.

My life was passing before my eyes. It's really amazing that they say that is what happens when you die, but I know for a fact that it also happens when you are about to die. When I was a young kid living at Medicine Lake, my father took me out to the dock that was floating about a mile from shore. I'm sure now it was only 100 feet, but when I got there and looked back it seemed like a mile. My dad was determined to teach me to swim. He picked me up and threw me off that float, in the direction of shore. I sank and swallowed a lot of lake water and I thought I was going to drown before he finally pulled me out. That event was being vividly projected again as I plummeted straight down. I also saw the tunnel of light, and I was heading for it at about 160 knots.

I looked down and there was nothing but jungle beneath me. All of sudden there was a small rice paddy right in the middle of all those trees. Then for absolutely no reason, the helicopter smoothed out, and we made a controlled crash on the ground. We were sliding in the mud, and I slammed both feet on the brakes, trying to make the aircraft stop. I ended up being the only casualty; by cutting my knees open on the dash. The Korean soldiers got out the back and formed a perimeter. Before long we had a bunch of helicopter coming in to pick us up, and arrange to haul our broken bird out. We got back to the unit and I headed for our club, where I pretty much stayed for the next three days.

Boeing engineers came around to talk to me about the crash and showed me pictures of the aft blades. Helicopter blades are made from honeycomb aluminum with a stainless steel spar that goes down the leading edge. All three blades impacted the tree and sheared off about three feet of the aluminum. The stainless steel spars were turned into shepherd hooks. They said that there was no way that the helicopter should have been able to fly as long as it did. With the blades so out of balance and bent the way they were, the entire aft section should have disintegrated. Boeing had no idea how we made it out alive. They said that a Chinook cannot sustain that kind of damage and still fly. The engineers explained that the two engines should have shaken their selves right off the airframe, and then the aft pylon, where the rotor blades are located, would have disintegrated. From that point, we probably would have tumbled end over end, until we became one with the earth.

This cat had now officially used up life number 9.

# FUCKING MEAT LOAF

As anyone who really knows me will attest, I will not eat very many things that come in a can. I had too many bad memories of my first tour. C rations continually. All of them in nice little cans. You ate them because you had to. There just were no other choices. When you are in the field day in and day out, you may not see a mess tent for quite some time. So you adjust by carrying C rats with you wherever you go. These will be your breakfast, lunch and dinner. For these reasons I also dislike TV dinners. If it's a meal in a box I have an instant aversion. This is why I really like a nice home cooked meal and won't have much to do with food that is, "Instant."

Now I was on my second tour and we did have a mess hall which served three meals a day, every day. The only problem was we had moved from C rations to B rats and some A rats. These meals are made from a large package which was canned, preserved or packaged. With the A rats you throw in some fresh food or perhaps something that is frozen or refrigerated. Sometimes the cooks would buy on the economy. They would head to the local village and pick up fresh fruit and vegetables. That was always a welcome treat.

Meals consisted of mystery meats with powdered eggs for breakfast. Sandwiches at lunch time, and then dinner which may be another type of meat, freeze dried potatoes and a canned vegetable. I'm not sure what it was or where it came from but it did resemble ground beef. I don't think it tasted too much like hamburger, but the cooks insisted that was what it was. The only way they knew how to prepare it was to mix it with water and other nutritious ingredients such as freeze dried onions and peppers. Throw in some instant eggs and left over bread. Then bake it until it turns hard, and serve it to the poor troops. We were told it was meat loaf. If you stood back, squinted your eyes and held your nose, you would swear it was the same thing your mother use to make. Wrong! I was always as hungry as the next guy, but even this was beyond description as a meal. But in order to maintain some type of weight and be able to respond to the rigors of war, you had to eat what was available. The big problem is that the cooks made enough meat loaf to feed an army, and the army didn't want to eat it. So in the morning for breakfast we had powdered eggs and the meat loaf. At lunch time we were provided with all the fixings for a sandwich, including the sliced concoction know as meat loaf. Then at dinner we had instant mashed potatoes, with a lovely mushy canned vegetable, and the addition of the protein of the day, meat loaf. If the Chef was school trained, then he would make gravy, and could now call the dinner, Swiss steak.

I remember one time the cook burned the meat loaf. It was dried out and tough and had the consistency of a presto log. Our cook took the gravy and kept adding powdered milk until it turned a light grey color. He then threw the gravy over the meat loaf. It went on the menu as the Friday night special, "Chicken Fried Steak." Sometimes this would go on for a week then we would get something else to eat, which may or may not have been chicken. Then it was back to the meat loaf. My wife just can't seem to understand why forty some years later I still will not allow her to make meat loaf. She craved it. I told her, "Hey! Let's go to Denny's or Marie Callenders and you can order all you can eat."

I also should have been suspicious of the warrant officer who had the additional duty as Mess Officer. You never, ever saw him in the mess hall eating with the rest of us. But at night you would pass by his room and you could smell him cooking something. I finally told him one time that maybe an investigation should be done on why he wasn't eating in the mess hall, and I got invited right in for dinner. He had a hot plate and a large black cast iron skillet, and he was sautéing onions and mushrooms. When they were done a steak went into the pan and got seared, and then the entire entrée was flipped onto two plates. Damn was that good. Of course he insisted he purchased all of this with his own money from the commissary in Qui Nhon. Looking back I realized how naïve I was, and what a conniving Mess Officer he was.

In order to make the meals more palatable we were convinced that we needed more nightly entertainment, and this could only mean one thing, "Women." We didn't have access to females, except for the hookers in the village, and most of us were married anyway, so that was out of the question.

What should we do? *"I know! Let's all chip in and send away for a, "Blow up Doll with Five Orifices." See! Right here it says it is made from the highest quality vinyl, and is completely washable".*

We clipped the coupon from the Field and Stream magazine someone was hiding, and then sent them a postal money order for shipping and packaging. I figured we would take care of the handling aspect once it arrived. No one could quite come to terms of usage of Ms. Orifice when and if she arrived, but we all agreed she would be our constant companion on field trips to the real O' Club. We waited two weeks for our package, and then waited some more. Finally we had to make up a duty roster so that every day, someone was assigned to make the walk to the unit postal point, and check for the package. When I left four months later Ms. "O" still hadn't arrived. I believe she was waylaid enroute and ended up married to a commission officer.

# PUSSY CAT

I did a lot of flying for the Koreans Tiger Division (ROK). As I mentioned, they provided security for Lane Army Airfield, and also conducted operations against the V.C and NVA. They had a reputation that they took great pains to perpetrate. If they received enemy fire from a village, they would then proceed to destroy the whole place. If they were fired upon or lord forbid, someone was wounded or died, then they would surround the area. Once the village or patch of jungle was contained, they would tighten the noose and kill everything that moved. Every building, goat, chicken, dog and water buffalo would be flattened. Hence Lane AAF never took incoming rockets or mortars. It was the only base camp I ever heard of that was left alone.

Sometimes on combat assaults just when you dropped the ramp into the rice paddy, some Korean soldier would decide he did not want to get off the Hook and join his pals in the jungle. Then a gun fight would ensue. You had a heavily armed private who has decided he ain't going on a walk in the jungle. The lieutenant or captain who is in charge, and who will lose face if this private doesn't get off the bird, was now moving into action. The Koreans took no prisoners including their own people. The Lt. or Capt. would simply draw their gun and either shoot the offender or attempt to. This resulted sometimes in a mini-revolt when the private's buddies decided to join him. Then the danger potential went way up. Thirty plus men all heavily armed, and you cannot tell who is on whose side. The door gunners would swing their M-60 machine guns inside the helicopter and threaten to kill everyone if they all didn't get off the helicopter. This made for some really hairy situations. It's bad enough having the enemy shoot at you, but having to worry about getting shot down by our allies, can become nerve racking.

One of our guilty little pleasures was conducted in the evenings. We would grab a beer or cocktail and sit out on the little patio behind our club. Below was the security company for the airfield and every evening they conducted physical fitness training (PT). The Koreans had a different set of values in their army. I had not done PT since flight school and I could not recall seeing anyone else doing it. I know the enlisted U.S soldiers were usually too busy humping in the jungle to be worried about doing sit-ups. Our crew chiefs and gunners worked a 12 hour day unless there was a major problem with the helicopters, and then they might work all night.

*"Hi guys. I'm your new captain. I'll be getting you up early to do the daily dozen. There is nothing like twenty five pushup to get the juices flowing."*

*"Well Capt. You had better make sure your door is locked tonight or you might end up with a surprise. The only thing you will be pushing up is daisies."*

The Korean Lt. would line up his platoon in full uniforms with packs and helmets and included weapons. A couple of the soldiers would also be carrying their mortars and base plates which probably weighted thirty pounds or so. They would start doing exercises like jumping jacks and pushups while the Lt. walked around with a 2x4 with a carved handle. It looked like a four foot long, square baseball bat. If a soldier dropped or could not finish his PT, the Lt. would start beating him with the 2x4, until he either got back up or until he could not move. Usually the platoon Sergeant would have to pull the Lt. off the offending man before permanent damage was done. Sure made me glad to be in the U. S. Army instead of the ROK.

Another little incentive for the Korean soldier, "To be all he could be", was that if they fell asleep while on guard duty and were caught, they were usually shot without so much as a: "Whoops! Don't do that." The Officer or Sergeant of the Guard would be out on the lines, creeping around. If they came across a guard who wasn't awake they would simply execute them on the spot. Made for a really tight military unit and a very alert guard force.

The ROK had soldiers in the field and of course we had to fly supplies out to them on a daily basis. Normally only one bird would get assigned to the food re-supply, and this presented a whole new set of circumstances for us pilots. The crew chief and gunners worked for me and as a warrant officer, I outranked them. But I was also responsible for their well being. It was their job to load the helicopter and it was my job to make sure I got everything I was supposed to. I then had to check the weight to make sure we could get the old freight wagon off the ground. In theory that is how the Army would like it to work. I sat through a lot of classes back at Ft.Wolters, and I don't recall a single one regarding being a, "Pimp Daddy." Maybe it was in the class on Health and Welfare.

Located about 100 yards east of the Korean logistics pad was a Vietnamese hut sitting out in a rice paddy. Inside were an old mama-san and her daughter "Pussy Cat", and three or four other children. I am not sure who they belonged to, or if they were in day care. "Pussy Cat" supplemented her income by providing a service to anyone who had cash. When we landed, the crew chiefs and gunners could not wait to head over for a quick visit, so us pilots would give them time off while we loaded the helicopter. This was a payback, from us to them. They took damn good care of us and the helicopters, and were up before us getting ready for the day's flights. They were also with the birds late into the evening, checking everything and repairing small problems. These men worked their butts off and rarely got the attention they deserved. Us two pilots, would hump all of the food and other sundries into the helicopter with the help of the ROK guys, while the crew chief and gunners got their ashes hauled by "Pussy Cat." I sure as hell wasn't going over there. I vividly remember the film in Basic Training where the guy's dick fell off.

One of the pilots who was a regular with me on these log runs was "The Virgin." He was kind of a nerdy looking guy who was maybe early 20s, and claimed he was saving himself for his bride, should he ever find one. The crew took it upon themselves to continually try and goad "Virg" into visiting "Pussy Cat" and getting his cherry popped. Finally one morning we were loading the Hook and the guys got a couple of beers into "Virg." The next thing I know, they have him heading across the rice paddy for the hooch. They came back a little later and lo and behold they said, "Virg" was no longer a virgin and:

"Gee Chief. It sure didn't take very long. His pants hit the floor and he was done." "Virg" could not quit smiling or talking about his new found experience, and now was volunteering to do the log re-supply runs every day. "Hey! You need someone to load 16 tons. I'm your man. Hell! Why don't I just run on over there and get started. You can bring the helicopter and crew whenever you get around to it."

"Virg" became a real pain in the ass because the crew was running off to visit "Pussy Cat" and "Virg", who should be helping me load the bird, is going with them. Not fair! Plus the crew was claiming that "Virg" was "in love" and hogging all the time with Ms Cat.

One fine morning I got the -47 loaded while everyone was gone across the rice paddy. The crew returned, but I waited and waited and no "Virg." Finally I had to get out of the cockpit and trudge across the field to drag "Virg" out of "Pussy Cat's" clutches. I got him up off the sleeping mat and dressed and out the door while "Pussy" is screaming in Vietnamese and I was sure, calling me nasty names. We got back and fired up the engines, and got ready to take off. In front of us out the cockpit window I saw "Pussy Cat" come out the front door of her hooch naked. She had an old iron bathtub in the front yard, and after a morning of rolling around with the troops she would hop into the tub, for a scrub.

I lifted the Hook off the pad and started my hover check to make sure I could fly with the load I had. I was also watching "Pussy" lying in the water. The Chinook helicopter is named after a northwest Indian word which means, "Big wind," and that baby could put out a breeze of over 100 m.p.h, when she was pulling a load off the ground.

As I started to lift off "Pussy Cat" was laying there, and she is giving me the, "One Finger Salute" which pissed me off. My crew has been contributing to the gross national income for her family, and this is how she returns the favor. So instead of climbing out I kept the helicopter low, and buzzed the bath tub and the hooch. Straw was flying everywhere from the roof and chickens and ducks were losing their feathers. This was looking like the scene from "The Wizard of Oz" when the tornado struck. Plus, I had managed to suck all the water from the tub and dumped it and "Pussy Cat" over in the rice paddy. There would be no more visits to "Pussy Cat" for a while and everyone was pissed at me. Especially "Virg." Maybe we'll get some work done now.

# THE FLYING WALENDAS

One of our other services for the ROK was to haul sling loads of ammo and boxes of large supplies. Everything would be loaded in large cargo nets, and then the Chinook would hover over the load to pick it up. A Korean soldier would stand on top of the load and hold a large canvas donut, that held the net closed. This would be looped over the cargo hook in the belly of the helicopter, and the crew chief would lie on the floor of the helicopter and give directions to the pilots. Right, left, up, down, back, or forward. Then the magic words, "You're hooked" and away we would go.

When you came into pick up a load, you always would key your F.M radio to dissipate the static electricity that built up. If you didn't, when the guy on the ground slapped the donut to the hook, the static charge could knock him off the load and on his ass. If that happened they would not get back on the loads, and you would have to land and drop off a gunner to take over. There was no way to get the gunner back on board, so they would have to spend the day with the Koreans. When we were done, we would come back and get them. Of course, sometimes you would get a ROK who would be giving you trouble all day by screwing up the loads, or not getting the donut set. Then of course it was all right to zap him.

This was boring work. Pick up a load, fly out and drop it. Go back and get another load. Repeat as necessary for six to eight hours. During these round robin log runs you had to pick up a load of nets which were all wrapped inside another net. These were taken back to the supply depot, and would then get re-loaded with supplies. There were only so many nets, so it was drop a load, pick up the empties, go back and start all over again.

One day we were talking big and bragging about our flying abilities when the challenge was thrown down. "I can take a load out, drop it and pick up a load of nets and return, faster than you can." The contest was on. We stuck the crew chief in the hole and told him what we were doing. The other pilot went first and did just fine. Come in and pickle the load. Move over to the pile of nets, while the crew chief is giving really fast instructions on where to move the helicopter. *"O.k. Sir. Forward a foot. Stop! Back and inch. Stop! Right a smidge. Erase the smidge and give me a Red Pubic Hair. Perfect!"*
Get the ROK to hook it fast and away you go. I went next and set a new standard, so now the co-pilot has to beat my time. We are having great fun and making the day just fly by.

Fourth trip and it's my turn again. I was jacked and was going to set the world record for drop offs and pickups. I came barreling in and dropped the load and zoomed over the nets. I knew exactly where to position the bird over the load, and the next thing I heard from the crew chief was, "Sir! You are hooked." I pulled everything this -47 had and leapt into the sky. We were climbing out past 500 feet and the crew chief was yelling at me, "We have to go back." I can't think of a reason for this and he clarifies by telling me, "The ROK is hanging onto the net, and he really should be back on the ground." I spun around and went back to drop off our passenger. Guess who didn't have a ROK for the rest of the day to hook up loads? I had to set down and off load a gunner to do the sling loads for the rest of the day. Now I had two pissed off people.

We spent a lot of time flying boring missions for the Koreans so we were always on the lookout for a way to have fun and make the time go by faster. When we flew loads of supplies to the LZ's out in the boonies, we always had a Korean soldier with us to act as an interpreter. This was necessary so that the interpreter could talk to the ground unit and find out where we were to drop the load, or where to sit down so we could be unloaded. These guys were fun to talk to and most were just privates, but everyone I ever had on my plane was college educated. Some even had advanced degrees, but this didn't keep them from being drafted and sent to Vietnam.

We were flying one day and I told the other pilot that I wanted him to distract the interpreter, who stood between us, while I switched on the auto pilot. This was a rudimentary device which just kept the -47 sort of flying straight and level. I then told my co-pilot that I wanted him to pretend that he was tired and finally nod off and take a nap. So he did. I waited about 10 minutes and then I started to nod off also. I kept my head going up and down and yawning and slapping myself. I then fell "asleep". The Korean went nuts. He shook me, then shook my co-pilot. Nothing he could do, would wake us up. Both of us were using maybe half of one eye to make sure we didn't fly into another helicopter, or a mountain. As we got near the LZ we simply woke up, turned off the autopilot, and landed the helicopter like nothing was going on. Sometimes the interpreter would leave and never get back on our plane. We would land and they would disappear, or they would just stand there and tell you that you're crazy, and they are not going to fly with you ever again.

One mission I hated was flying the weekly load of Kim chi out to the fire bases. Kim chi is cabbage that is mixed with garlic and spices, and then put into large pots or jars and left to ferment. I think that they just wait until it is rotten, and then it's ready to eat. We would stack this stuff to the ceiling, and you had no idea how bad it smelled. I get nauseous just thinking about it. Usually the interpreter was standing between us, and you just know he had a bowl full for breakfast. So not only did the plane stink, this guy's breath could set your mustache on fire. So our only course of action was, that one pilot would wear a gas mask, while the other pilot sat way up in his seat and stuck his head out the window. With the gas mask on you couldn't see shit, so one pilot had to keep the tears out of his eyes to guide the helicopter.

The Kim chi was bad but didn't compare to the Vietnamese Nuoc Mam. This was fish sauce made from sardines or other fish, salt and garlic. It was put into large vats and left to liquefy. I remember the first time I flew over a Nuoc Mam factory and entered the cloud hovering over the building. I thought I was going to die. I started gagging, and was pretty sure I was going to puke all over myself, and the floor of the helicopter. Of course the crew chief would have made me clean it up, and then rush to tell everyone about the sissy pilot. Army Aviation sure was glamorous.

We did have one perk though. The Korean Army was big on entertaining their troops. They would find a band, and hire some girls as eye candy and to sing. Before the ladies got to Nam, the Koreans sent them to Hong Kong for a new set of titties. Silicone implants were just coming into their own, and the Koreans wanted to make sure their troops didn't go AWOL. If you got the show mission, you picked up the band and the girls first thing in the morning, and then flew them from fire base to fire base all day long. They would get out and put on a show for an hour or so, then load back up and head for the next place. A lot of times we got our own special show during the flights. The band would crank up in the back and the girls would put on head sets and sing to us over the intercom, *"Rouy Rouy. Me gotta go"* or the ever popular, *"Rollypop."* Some of the pilots even let the girls sit in their laps and do a little steering. *"Here! Let me hold those plastic things out of the way so you can drive my helicopter better."* It's in the manual. warrant officer pilots should always try to be helpful to the passengers.

The ROK army was big on showing their appreciation to the pilots who flew the show missions, and would invite them over to the headquarters for a dinner party. If they wanted to show special thanks to a pilot, that pilot would find a key under his dinner plate. The key number would correspond to a room number, and the room would contain a girl from the show troupe. She performed a solo song and dance, or so I was told.

# LIFE IN THE WILD

Being a Chinook pilot in the 196th sure beat hell out of being a scout pilot in the 1st Cav. I had my own room with an air conditioner, and I had a small refrigerator, just in case it was too far to walk to the bar. I pretty much flew from sun up to sun down, but stayed home at night.

Another great perk were the jeeps. Our T.O.E (table of organizational equipment) said we would be issued a jeep for the commander, a jeep for operations, a jeep for maintenance, and one for the First Sergeant. This probably added up to four or five jeeps for the unit. In reality we had jeeps coming out our ass. The pilots probably had an additional half dozen jeeps sitting around for whoever needed to use one. Every single one of them was stolen.

One of our little, illegal missions would be to fly down to Qui Nhon Army Base. There were all these military units with a supporting Post Exchanges, hospital, Commissary, and supply depots. We would go on a re-con and find a jeep that was unlocked, and then simply borrow it. These jeeps did not have keys to operate them. You just turned on the ignition and drove off. The driver of the jeep was suppose to chain the steering wheel to a bracket welded to the floor and close it with a lock, but G.I.s being the lazy people they are, just couldn't be bothered. So we would grab the jeep and drive it back to the Chinook, and up the ramp into the cargo compartment. By the time we got to Lane AAF the crew chief had the bumper repainted with our unit numbers, and some lucky pilot now had his own transportation. Whoever was going to be the new proud owner was responsible for filing off the serial numbers. When the jeeps got wrecked or simply quit running we would abandon them and go find another.

Jimmy Pratt left on a mission to Qui Nhon for the procurement of a jeep. It took his crew about two minutes to come up with one that had been left unlocked. It was immediately driven up the ramp of the CH-47 and the transformation began. The Chinook then departed Qui Nhon for Phu Cat Air Force Base. The jeep was off loaded at Phu Cat and driven away by some air force personnel who returned a few minutes later with a speed boat sitting on a trailer. The boat was taken to the Korean headquarters where it became part of the in-country R & R center.

I remember one night when a bunch of us went to the main Officers Club and I drove my semi official; "WO-2, Assistant Ops Officer, Bar Manager, Lets Party, jeep." When we went I think there were four or five of us. When we left the club to return home I believe I had about eight on board. I remember two guys were sitting on the hood, and the rest were sprawled wherever. Now a jeep can go by road or it can go cross country. I went cross country because that is a lot more fun. Everything at Lane was terraced. So I had to go down some hills and then cross the main road and start going up hills toward our place. It was go down a hill. Cross a flat spot. Go down a hill cross a flat spot. Then I hit the main road through the post and started up. Go up a hill. Cross a flat spot. Go up a hill. Cross a flat spot. There must have been a half dozen of each. We were about half way home when the two guys on the hood disappeared. One minute they were there, and the next second they were gone. I came to a halt and we all got out to look for them. They were found laying in the dirt, half conscious. Some dumb, son of a bitch put a clothes line up right on the trail I was using. It snagged both of these guys and damn near took their heads off as it flipped them off the jeep. If they hadn't been all lousy goosy from being drunk it would have killed them.

We also use to drive the supply depots crazy by stealing things we needed like a refrigerator; a couple of air conditioners; or a load of lumber. We had some talented crew members who could paint rather well. So the rear pylon of a Chinook would be treated to a quick paint job showing the 1st Cav. patch on one side and the 101st Airborne eagle on the other. The crew chief and gunner would walk into the large supply depot and find what we needed and rig it for sling load. Then the Chinook would appear and haul the goodies off. The supply people would swear, depending on where they were standing, that either a Cav. or a Screaming Eagle -47 stole the stuff. We didn't do this often, but when we did it was a work of art.

Our midnight requisition process was too successful. Our unit had an abundance of rotor blades, engines, transmissions, tools, batteries, lubricants, and assorted spare parts. Word would come down that we were going to be inspected to make sure we were incompliance with regulations. The entire unit would start hiding things all over the base. Holes were dug and filled with boxes containing all the above mentioned items, then covered up. Jeeps were scattered around the other units, hopefully to be retrieved later. Dummy missions were assigned, and whole loads were transported by helicopters, elsewhere. Then after the inspection all of these efforts had to be reversed. What a pain in the patootie.

# IT'S ALL FUN UNTIL SOMEONE LOSES AN EYE

Flying a Chinook brought you the chance to also do bombing missions. We would pick up these huge rubber blivets which contained 500 gallons of water, or a water trailer with 1000 gallons. The load was supposed to go to a unit out in field or at a fire base. The rules were very clear. If a sling load started to oscillate and present a danger to the aircraft, then the pilot could pickle the load. If you were flying along with your water container hanging below the belly, and you passed over a village that you may have received fire from on some occasion. You just might experience an oscillation that required you to bomb the village. The load would get pickled and the entire crew would watch it heading for the grass huts. When it hit it was like a small tsunami. Depending on how well your seat of the pants bomb site was, you could possibly take out one or two huts, or drown a water buffalo.

This also held true for the O-1 bird dog airplane owned and operated by the U.S Air Force. If one got shot down or crashed landed, we would send a Hook in to recover it. And of course the rules are the rules. So heading back to the Air Force base with one hanging below the -47, they would sometimes start to "fly" on their own. You might be looking out the window and all of sudden this O-1 was right alongside of you. The engine may not be working but there is still lift in those wings. Nothing to do but "pickle it." After hitting the little red button that caused disconnect, I would begin a turn so everyone could watch this plane fly off on its own. The bird dog would start to spin and spiral right into an eventual crash. There would be one more crater in a rice paddy. There was never enough left of the O-1 to go back for.

Nights in the Chinook lounge were events in and of themselves. A good friend was Jimmy Pratt who had also been in the 1st Cav. at the same time as I was, and was on his second tour in Nam. The guys who were there on their first tours took great pleasure in calling me and Jimmy "Baby killers", so it was only natural that we would retaliate. Jimmy and I would wait for the guilty party to get drunk and go sleepy bye, and then we would make our move. We were so bent on revenge we were even known to buy the victim drinks. I put the drinks on the victim's page in the book anyway, so it was double payback. The offender would wake up in the morning and look in the mirror, to find a 1st Cav. patch inscribed on their forehead in magic marker. You would see them the later at breakfast with a raw patch of skin, where they had been scrubbing with Ajax. It usually took about a week for the marking to finally wear off. And unless someone told them, they were also walking around with a giant Cav. patch covering their backs. "Damn! Were we mature, or what?"

Our Officers hooch was in the form of a large U. In the middle of the U we had a volley ball court set up, and there was usually a game or two each week. Sides would be chosen and drinks consumed and normally you played one handed, so as not to spill your beer or cocktail. The game was "combat rules" which simply meant, there are no rules. You could hit over the net, under the net, beside the net, or through the net. As long as the ball was in the air it was considered in play. If you wanted to score a point this meant you could go over the net, under the net, or around the net, to place a hit on your opponent, who may or may not have the ball. This resulted in injuries, which sometimes were to the extent that a pilot could not fly the next day. This tended to really piss off the Operations Officer and the commander, so they were always trying to ban the games. Try telling drunk pilots in Vietnam that they can't do something. *"What are you going to do? Send me to Vietnam? Put me in a war zone? Get me shot at?" Worthless threats.*

We got so good at volley ball we got stupid. We made the mistake of challenging the Koreans to a contest. They showed up and the games began. I think by the time we finished playing them, they were spotting us nineteen or twenty points, and still beating us. Damn! Did we look foolish, and never made that mistake again. How come no one in our group was smart enough to remember that volley ball was the Korean national sport?

Friday and Saturday nights were often spent at the Lane AAF Officers Club. They would bring in a band once in awhile to entertain the troops, so we would load up in our stolen jeeps and drive over. You could drink cheap and also order a steak dinner for a couple of bucks. I had this great friend named Ricky, who was on his second tour and flying Cobras for the gun company. Ricky and I had spent our first tour together, and were also at Rucker at the same time when I went through Chinook transition. He was a great pilot, but a little crazy when he was drunk. We had Vietnamese bar girls at the O' club and of course they had their own outdoor bathroom facilities. These were built to the same specifications as the G.I.s facilities. This meant that they were a standalone building with a trap door in the rear to access the cut in half 55 gal. barrels. Above the barrels was a plank seating area with holes cut out to sit on. We would be in the club drinking and carrying on when you would hear a scream followed by a string of loud Vietnamese words. Then the bar girl would come in rubbing her crotch and yelling. All the other girls would gather around and jabber back and forth, while shooting eye darts at Ricky. It was only too clear by the look on their faces, what they would like to do to him.

 Ricky would watch for a bar girl to get ready to leave out the back, and he would race out and open the trap door on the shitter. He would slide the barrel out, and crawl in and lay on his back waiting. The unsuspecting bar girl would come out to use the facility and would stand over the hole, and then squat down to relieve herself. Ricky would then poke them in the privates with a stick. The girls hated him and he could never get one to wait on him.
I wonder why?

The days drug on with flight missions hither and yon, and the only thing to look forward to was the nights. Going home just was not an option, until Uncle Sugar told you your time was up.

# F.U.I

*It's just like D.U.I but you are a little higher off the ground.*

I had a friend named Dave Helton who introduced me to Chivas Regal. Dave was a CW-3 when he and I flew together in the 196th and we spent many a night sitting in our little bar together. Dave went on to become a very senior CW-4 and then Master Warrant. He ran the school at Ft. Rucker for the Master Warrant program and was my mentor when I went through that course thirty years later. I was fortunate to have him present when I was promoted to CW-5.

I could purchase a fifth of this scotch for about $3, so it was cheap and easy to get a little shit faced at night. Easier than facing the demons waiting for you in your room. Dave and I would sit around our little club most nights and drink the Chivas until it was gone. This may be 1:00 a.m. or it might be 5:00 a.m. It all depended upon how much of the world chaos we were correcting, or what our current plans were for ending the war.

Dave and I were sitting in the club one night drinking our scotch when we noticed a crack around the bottom of the Chivas bottle. We began to examine this crack, when we noticed that it wasn't really a crack, but looked as if someone had broken the bottom off and re-glued it. We got another bottle down and checked it and found the same un-explained, glued bottom. I got behind the bar and looked at some other high end booze and noticed the same occurrence. The next day we contacted the military police, and told them that we had found all these bottles, which appeared to have had the bottoms cut off and re-glued. They took a report and said they would get back to us. A couple of weeks later, I was informed that the Army Criminal Investigators had broken up a group that had been stealing high priced liquor, and re-selling it on the black market. The way the scam worked was that the shipments coming over by boat would spend about thirty days at sea. While cruising toward Vietnam the crew would cut off the bottoms of expensive booze and put it in large containers. Then they would do the same with the cheap stuff. The crew would then swap the contents and re-glue the bottoms.

Now the cheap stuff would be sold as high end merchandise to the army. The expensive liquor would go to army clubs where the managers would pay a cut rate. Then it got marked up and sold as premium and they split the profits. The army clubs in Vietnam were rife with fraud. A lot of sergeants got caught ripping off the system. They did everything from the booze substitutions to rigging the slot machines that every club had. The club managers would rig the slots so that they either never paid off or paid off a small amount. Then they would re-rig the machines and let one of their friends play. It would not be long before a large jackpot was hit, and the two of them would split the winnings.

Dave and I would finish the bottle off and either go to bed or go flying. Sometimes but not often we would simply ride down the hill to the flight line, and crawl into our seats in the helicopter ready for that days missions. The Chinooks were protected from mortar and rocket blasts by high walls that were on both sides of the helicopter. When you landed on our runway you would taxi down to your assigned revetment, turn left and park between the walls. In the morning when you were ready to fly your missions, you were required to lift the nose of the Hook straight up while the rear wheels remained on the ground. You then had to fly out of the revetment without hitting the sides. It took a very steady hand, or you just closed your eyes and hoped for the best. It you banged the bird on the walls, you had to buy the crew chief a case of beer, but even with this incentive for free booze, the chiefs didn't like their planes getting dinged.

We would pre-flight the helicopter under the watchful eye of the crew and then we would strap in and start the engines. If the chief didn't like the looks of us two pilots, due to excessive alcohol intake, then up would come cans of cold beer. The crew usually kept a six pack or two in the water coolers in the back for in flight emergencies, and a couple of shit faced pilots, trying to take off between two high walls, was classified as an emergency.

This also led to other problems due to our warped sense of humor. Once we got airborne we would take a load out to the grunts in the bush. Normally this would be a sling load of artillery rounds or maybe a new cannon. The G.I. in the field lived in holes where they slept and fought from. I would come in with a load and start blowing everything they owned all over the LZ. Once I had dropped the load and started to pull back up, I would open my side window and throw a couple of empty beer cans out. I know the guys in the holes loved us, and were kidding when they aimed their M-16s at us. I'm sure they were pretending  they were going to shoot us down.

# THE LONE STRANGER AND TONTO

We had civilian technicians from the Boeing Company living with us. Their job was to insure that the helicopters were properly maintained and that we got all the parts and equipment that we needed. They also got the bulletins with the latest upgrades and modification for our helicopters.

One of the techs was always wandering around pissing and moaning and crying in his beer. He had been involved with a group of friends, who had gone to Alaska. They contacted him and wanted him to invest with them in some place called the North Slope. They thought they could find oil there, but were not sure. He passed. Now a year or so later they continually wrote him letters telling him how much money they were making, and how much he was not making. Talk about a man with a bad attitude.

There was also an Indian who was a technician on the CH-47 power plants. This man was always drunk and thought nothing of getting on his motor scooter and driving from Lane to Qui Nhon. This could be on a quiet afternoon or after the sun went down. No one could ever figure how he kept from being shot by one side or the other, as he sped down the road to town. Maybe the fact that he owned a bar and whore house in Qui Nhon had something to do with it. It was probably a V.C R&R center.

One night he was drunker than usual and started roaming around the living quarters carrying a submachine gun. He insisted he had enemies, and he was going to kill them. He just had to find them first. Things started to get real scary when he fired off a few rounds. Everyone ran for cover and we all hid. Pilots were under their bunks or in their closets. A couple of guys ran out to the volley ball court and tried to bury themselves in the sand. Nobody wanted to confront this mad man, and try and get his gun away. The military police were called and they figured they didn't want to become involved, "Because that Indian is a civilian and we have no jurisdiction".

The medics were called next and two of them came up to our house on the hill, loaded with syringes. These needles contained enough tranquillizers to put down a horse, and they just had to stick the crazy Indian without getting shot. The medics hid out. One was in a hallway broom closet and the other was in the showers. They tried to peek out and see if the Indian was around, but he never showed himself. Finally everyone heard him fire up his motor scooter and roar off down the hill, heading for the main gate. He made it to town again, but he had used up his welcome with us, and was transferred back to the U.S.A.

# IN THE WIND

I was scheduled to finish my tour of duty in January 1970, and at that time I would also finish my obligation to the U.S. Army. In December I was called into the commanders' office and told that I was being offered the chance to take a direct commission to 1st Lieutenant. This would move me from the specialized field of a Warrant Officer Helicopter Pilot, to that of a real officer with more responsibilities and more work. As a Lt. I would have additional duties to perform and flying would be my secondary job. Officers were assigned to a branch of the service such as Infantry or Artillery and they would have to go to school to become trained in that area. They could keep flying, but not nearly as much, and sometimes not at all.

This promotion also entailed an extension of one year, most of which would be spent right where I was in Vietnam. The main reason for the offer was so that the Army could retain the pilots who were trained and keep them in the service, and it would bolster the Officer Corp. A lot of young lieutenants had finished their obligations to the Army and were getting out of the service.

I informed the commander that I would need time to make my choice. At the very least I needed to confer with Heleen and get her input. This was a big decision for several reasons. First. Would be the fact that I would remain in Vietnam for at least another year. I had a wife and two children at home and had not spent much time with any of them.

Second. I would have a new commitment to the U. S. Army. Instead of going home and staying put, I would have to go to school somewhere for several months. Then it would be an assignment anywhere in the world where they needed a new Lt. Lastly. At that point I would probably stay in the army and make it a twenty year career. That was not all bad, as I would be eligible to take full retirement at age thirty-nine, with all of the benefits. I just had to ask my family if they didn't mind staying in the military and moving every couple of years, somewhere new.

The commander told me that the decision was on the table and there would not be a chance for me to confer with Heleen. I had to make the decision right then and there. Based on all the uncertainty I told him that I was not going to take the commission and that I would rotate home when my current tour was up. At that point I had about two weeks remaining, before I would become a civilian again.

We had a neat little ceremony for each pilot that lived long enough to go home. On your final day in the unit they would load you up in the Chinook, for your flight to the departure Air Force base. The crew chiefs would strap smoke grenades to the rear ramp, and when the time was right they would pull the pins. The Hook would take off and then make a turn to fly low level across the airfield and over the unit. They would drop the ramp and pull the pins, and everyone would come out to wave bye bye to the lucky guy going home. The last part of the flight was a soaring climb up and over our little Officer's Club.

My turn arrived and it was a little emotional. When you spend every day in combat with the same guys you get pretty attached to them. As much as you want to go home, you have this feeling of abandoning them. It's really conflicting. But in spite of this I packed and kissed everyone good bye, and took my turn being honored in the fly-by. Two days later I was home with Heleen and the girls, and a civilian once more.

Thirty days later I was a cop, but that's another book.

## About the Author

Michael served two tours of duty in Vietnam as a combat helicopter pilot. He flew in the Army for seven years and was an instructor. He remained in the US Army Reserves and retired after twenty eight years. While in the USAR he participated in numerous Protective Service Missions around the world. Michael became a PSM Instructor and trained various law enforcement personnel. He was also an Anti-Terrorism Driving Instructor.

Michael served as an officer in the Tacoma Police Department and retired as a Detective in the Homicide unit. He spent a total of thirty years in law enforcement and retired from the Division of Fraud for the State of Washington.

He has three children and two grandchildren, and is living in Arizona.

See what other books and projects Michael is working on. Visit him at: www.mdlazaresauthor.com

Made in the USA
Middletown, DE
29 August 2016